The Blue Print

The Keys to Making **BIG** Money in Professional Sales

REGGIE MARABLE

Published by:

FriesenPress

Suite 300 — 852 Fort Street
Victoria, BC, Canada V8W 1H8

www.friesenpress.com

Distributed to the trade by The Ingram Book Company

Table of Contents

PART 4: Managing the Sales Process

PART 5: Successful Ways to Manage Your Business

Being the CEO of Your Own Personal Enterprise

PART 6: Summary of the Blue Print Fundamentals

APPENDIX: THE BLUE PRINT EXPERIENCE

REAL LIFE SUCCESS STORIES

ACKNOWLEDGMENTS

First and foremost, I would like to thank my loving and supportive family. My wonderful wife and best friend, April, has been a constant source of inspiration throughout my professional career. Her unwavering belief in my ability to succeed provides an extra energy boost during all of my tough days. I am blessed to have two awesome children (Kennedy-6 & Chase-4) that have unconditional love for their Daddy and view me as their Superman. Holding their bright future in my hands provides never ending motivation!

I would like to thank my parents for instilling work ethic, pride, confidence, humility, and discipline in the core of my soul. They taught me that I can accomplish anything with faith in God, hard work, and belief in my talent. I would like to thank my older brother Rodney for setting an elite standard for his little brother. You inspired me to reach for the stars!

I would like to thank my Morehouse brothers — *Kwende Jones (#53) for the "free" legal advice and Keith Turner (#30) for the "free" web-site design and guidance throughout this long process. I sincerely appreciate your motivation to complete this project!*

I would like to thank everyone instrumental to my career progression at Sprint — *Wanda Satryb for hiring a college kid into corporate America and keeping me on the right path (I still remember you telling me to tuck my shirt in), Brian Nagel for allowing me to tag-along and learn the art of sales when I was an engineer, Jim King for taking a chance on an engineer with no sales experience, Ken Exum for being an awesome sales coach and helping me blossom into an elite sales professional, Mike Lanwehr for giving me my first shot in sales leadership, and Carolyn Rehling for providing me with the opportunity to demonstrate my capabilities at the executive level. Finally, I would like to thank John Dupree for wisdom and guidance throughout the years as my mentor!*

I would like to thank all of my colleagues at Sprint for their continued guidance and support throughout this long journey — *Carolyn Rehling for being an awesome mentor and pushing me to complete this project, John Dupree for navigating me through the Sprint review process and writing an EXCEPTIONAL foreword, Steve Funk for the legal advice, and all of the*

wonderful folks that took time to provide input to enhance my manuscript —
Steve "The Professor" Smetana, Paul Reese, Brian Nagel, Angel Joshua, Lacie
Garrett-Noe, and Mark Bonavia.

I would like to thank the original **BIG MONEY** team in Atlanta that
helped to make the **Blue Print** a reality — *Lacie Garrett-Noe, Moe Ilyas,*
Jon Nelson, Kevin Nixon, Joey Polk, Jamie Brady, Lisa Barber, Betsy Cowart,
Kelly McGee, Regi Pruitt, Jay "The Jedi Master" Patel, Jim Vose, Nathan
Smith, Darlene Weaver, and Michael Hamilton. We dominated the Atlanta
market and built the **#1** sales team at Sprint! I will always cherish our
special connection.

Finally, I would like to thank all of the talented and fearless sales professionals on my current team, **BIGGER MONEY**, in North Texas,
Oklahoma, Arkansas, and Louisiana. You are the BEST sales team in the
entire company and I'm very fortunate to work with such a special group
of talented people!

Sky is the limit...

FOREWORD

John Dupree
Senior Vice-President of Business Sales
Sprint Corporation

Sales may not be the oldest profession but it is an enduring one in its own right. Lots of people have engaged in it, some successfully, but many others with only a sense of frustration that they had the wrong product, the wrong price, the wrong territory, the wrong everything to make it a career. Yet all too often it is not the product, or the price, or any single external situation that derails a sales career; it is the inability of the salesperson to consistently build the skills and intentionally engage in the activities that will, over time, give him the very best chance to succeed. Professional sales is not for everyone, and lucky is the prospective salesperson that discovers early on that his interests lay elsewhere and makes the change. But for those who are truly committed to beginning a professional sales career, or for those already in sales who want to earn and grow yet may not have seen the success they had hoped for, then Reggie Marable's **<u>Blue Print</u>** is required reading.

I have known and worked with Reggie for a number of years and seen him take teams and build winning professionals through the use of a disciplined, passionate approach to selling and to personal development. The **<u>Blue Print</u>** was co-authored over the years by demanding sales management, uninterested prospects, hard to read buyers, skeptical team members, and recalcitrant customers of all sorts. It is punctuated, however, by smiles, handshakes, contracts, commissions and success. Nothing in the **<u>Blue Print</u>** is theoretical; this book describes winning practices that have repeated themselves in numerous situations across many teams over a number of years.

Effort matters. If there is one thing you will walk away from the **<u>Blue Print</u>** with, it is that simple truth. Some individuals may have more pleasing personalities, others may be smarter or more naturally gifted in one component of the selling process or another, but without consistent work and an investment of time and effort, sales results will simply disappear. You might not sense that from the titles of so many sales leadership books where the "secret" of this, or the "power" of that, beckon the salesperson like a magic talisman with the lure of mystical selling incantations. That is not the **Blue Print**. There is no magic here; rather something far better.

This book is very simply, a plan. Because though effort matters, it is investing that effort in the right things, the right way, at the right time that produces compounded results. A great many skilled and committed building contractors, if given the proper blueprint, can construct a beautiful, functional edifice. Yet even the most gifted natural builders would have difficulty doing so without the guidelines and instruction of an architect who knew what he was doing. What Reggie provides in the **Blue Print** is the plan for building a successful sales career, a plan that he has used countless times with a wide variety of individuals. If you do not have the willingness to put in the time and energy to building your career then put this book down and move on; it will be of no use. But if you can commit the effort and the passion to professional sales, then the **Blue Print** will show you, in detail, how to turn that commitment into income and success. The great thing about the **Blue Print** is precisely that it isn't magic. With so many salespeople desperately looking for this season's quick fix or that "secret" to sales success, an individual who commits to the **Blue Print** sets himself apart from his competition in a way that will have lasting impact on his entire career.

For the habits we develop early on in our sales careers are the very same habits we will exhibit as senior salespeople or sales managers. Adopting the lessons of the **Blue Print** now will make you successful and generate income from your sales efforts, but more importantly, it creates the foundation from which you can build a fruitful career in sales and sales management. Reggie Marable has rolled out the plans clearly and in detail; all that's left is for you to undertake the job.

Are you ready to commit to the Blue Print?

PROLOGUE
Why You Should Read This Book

*"If people only knew how hard I work to gain my mastery,
it wouldn't seem so wonderful at all."*

- Michelangelo, Italian Artist -

Very simple….If you have aspirations to make **BIG MONEY** and become a top performer on a consistent basis, this book is for you! The **Blue Print** is a combination of successful tactics, strategies, and activities that will vastly increase your income, help you dominate the profession of sales, and advance your career in corporate America.

I started my career at Sprint right out of college in customer service taking in-bound calls in a call center. Over the years, I created, refined, and executed the **Blue Print** to dominate professional sales and climb the corporate ladder at Sprint. With hard work and a game plan, I ascended to an Executive level position responsible for a four state geography, 80+ sales professionals, and over $300,000,000 in revenue in less than 13 years from that call center. My **Blue Print** can be duplicated in your career to accomplish similar results!

The **Blue Print** transformed me into an elite performer as a Direct Sales Rep and helped me build the #1 sales team in the entire company as a branch manager. To validate this statement, here are a few of my accomplishments using the **Blue Print** as a direct sales representative:

- 2005 Total Earnings on a base salary of $40,000 — **$240,000**

- 2005 President's Club — *finished #4 in the entire company out of 3,000+ direct sales reps*

- 2004 President's Club — *finished #3 in the entire company out of 3,000+ direct sales reps*

- Selected by Sprint's senior leadership team to attend a fast track Executive Management Program for top performers identified as future leaders at Sprint

From a sales leadership perspective, my **Blue Print** will impact the performance of the sales reps on your team and increase the money in your bank account. After achieving phenomenal results in direct sales, I was promoted into sales leadership. In 2006, I assumed responsibility for one of the lowest performing sales branches at Sprint. This team was at 59% of quota and filled with a group of under-achieving sales professionals that did not possess the willingness or ability to win. I was given the responsibility to manage the under-performers out of the business and build a new team from scratch. I hired nine new sales professionals from different walks of life. My new team ranged from young adults right out of college with zero sales experience to mature professionals from other industries looking to dive into professional sales. I taught them the **Blue Print** and led by example. Within 3 years, we built a winning sales team that delivered elite results during a difficult corporate merger, two significant internal reorganizations that drastically impacted business operations, and a challenging economic environment. Using the **Blue Print**, we dominated the Atlanta business market and became the **#1** sales team at Sprint (*out of 300+ sales teams across the company*)!

If you implement the **Blue Print**, my results can be easily eclipsed by the sales team you personally lead! Here is a summary of my achievements as a Sales Manager using the **Blue Print**:

- Led the **#1** sales team at Sprint out of 350+ direct sales teams — 2008

- Produced the **#1** direct sales rep at Sprint out of 3,000+ reps — 2008

- Achieved President's Circle as a Sales Manager — 2008

- Average sales rep on my team made **$114,000** — *average of nine Sales Reps with base salaries under $40,000*

- Produced four President Circle Winners — *elite recognition for sales reps finishing in the top 5%*

- 88% Participation Rate — *eight out of nine account executives finished above 100% of Sales Quota*

- Selected by Sprint's senior executive team to attend an exclusive Leadership Program for top managers identified as senior executives in waiting

Today, I'm a Regional Sales Director, responsible for Sprint's direct sales force in North Texas, Oklahoma, Arkansas, and Louisiana. When I started this position, this territory was one the worst performing areas in the company (*there are 21 total geographic areas at Sprint*). In my current role, the **Blue Print** has produced the following results:

- Inspired **80+** Sales Professionals across four states to believe in and execute the **Blue Print** on a daily basis

- Revitalized the team's culture by injecting new energy and enthusiasm across the entire sales organization

- In less than 18 months, transformed this four state territory into one of Sprint's top performing areas

- Hit sales quota for **14** CONSECUTIVE months — *through July 2012*

- Hit sales quota **29** out of the past **30** months — *through July 2012*

- Managed 82 non-performers out of the business to allow for an influx of new talent

- Hired 71 new, talented, hungry, aggressive sales reps and trained them to believe and execute the **Blue Print** on a daily basis

- Appointed by our Senior Executives to lead several significant corporate initiatives to change the sales culture and revitalize our new hire training program

- Received Sprint's **Leadership Excellence Award** for dramatically improving sales results in a significantly under-performing geography — *Sprint's **Leadership Excellence Award** is the highest level of recognition for extraordinary directors, vice presidents and senior executives at Sprint whose contributions have made a significant impact to the business*

In summary, my **Blue Print** has a proven track record of success. It will revolutionize the way you sell, how you manage your business, and increase the money in your personal bank account! If you are interested in becoming a top performer, climbing the corporate ladder, and completely dominating the profession of sales, keep reading!

The Blue Print

PART 1
Introduction to the **Blue Print**

Chapter 1
Why Did I Create the **Blue Print**?

"What does not destroy me, makes me stronger."

- Friedrich Nietzsche, German philosopher—

It was 7:30 AM on a routine Monday morning. I was sitting in my car and wondering if I had the energy to make it through another day. My motto in life is *"Failure is NOT an Option."* However, for the first time in my life, I could sense failure. As I sat in the empty parking lot of our sales office, I stared out of my car window and began to cry...

It was month six of my first year in professional sales. I was struggling to generate sales activity and was on the verge of failure. The pressure to deliver sales results, requirement to make numerous "cold calls," and dealing with constant rejection throughout the day had broken my spirit and shattered my confidence. I had finally reached my breaking point.

Up to this point in my life, I had been successful in everything from sports to academics. I was a captain of my high school football team, homecoming king, earned a full football scholarship to college, graduated cum laude, and played professional football. I was a rising star at Sprint and clearly on the fast track. The stakes were high and I was on the verge of complete failure in professional sales. If I failed in this role, everyone would forget about all of my previous success. I would be fired and out in the streets searching for employment. Everyone's last memory of Reggie Marable would be the guy that failed at professional sales.

As I stopped crying, I pulled myself together and made a personal commitment to give my **Blue Print** thirty more days before pulling the plug on professional sales and moving back into a support role before I lost my job. Tasting failure for the first time in my life was the primary motivation for creating the **Blue Print**.

My normal routine was to arrive in the office before our Monday morning staff meeting and make a minimum of thirty five cold calls (*the best time to reach C-Level decision-makers is between 7:30 AM — 9:00 AM and after 5:00 PM*). As I sat in the parking lot, I picked up my cell phone and cold called the Chief Information Officer (CIO) of one of the largest manufacturing companies in Georgia. I had been targeting this company for months with little progress. I sent the CIO several emails, left numerous voice mail messages, and even stopped by his office in person on several occasions with a creative gift. Since I called at 7:35 AM, his administrative assistant was not in the office yet and this time **HE ANSWERED THE PHONE**! When I heard his voice, I almost dropped the phone in complete surprise. I was nervous but ready...I knew this was my shot!

> *"Luck is what happens when preparation meets opportunity."*
>
> *- Seneca, Roman Philosopher -*

Here is a summary of the conversation that changed the course of my professional career:

Reggie — *Good Morning. This is Reggie Marable from Sprint. How are you today?*

CIO — *I'm great. What can I do for you?*

Reggie — *You are the most important prospect in my sales territory and I'm very excited to have an opportunity to chat with you live. I've attempted to contact you on several occasions and hope you had a chance to review the information I sent via email and hand-delivered to your office. I'm confident Sprint can help your company gain more productivity from your mobile work force and secure a competitive advantage in the manufacturing industry. The purpose of my call is to schedule a brief meeting to determine how Sprint can be a resource to you. How about 10 AM on Thursday morning?*

CIO — *Hi Reggie. I've been meaning to call you back but I've been super busy. Thanks for the really cool gifts and meaningful information! I really appreciate your persistence and tenacity. Your timing is impeccable. One of my key initiatives is arming our mobile workforce with the ability to place orders and check inventory while they are in the field. Is this something you can help with?*

Reggie — *ABSOLUTELY! We have a vast portfolio of solutions that can help your company accomplish those goals and gain more productivity from your mobile workforce. I would love to meet in person to learn more about this strategic initiative. How about this Thursday at 10 AM? Also, what other stake holders at your company are part of this project? I would love to include them in our meeting to ensure we capture their requirements.*

CIO — *Great suggestion! I will make sure our VP of Sales and our VP of Operations are both in the meeting along with my IT Director. 10 AM sounds great. I look forward to meeting you in person*

This cold call resulted in an incredible sale that generated over **$1,000,000** of new revenue for Sprint. Our team designed a unique solution that allowed this company to increase the overall productivity of their mobile workforce. It jump-started my professional career in sales and gave me the confidence to pursue and close many more large deals.

I am sharing my **Blue Print** because I **NEVER** want another sales professional to experience the confusion, heartache, and tears I endured during my first year of professional sales. In 2003, I was a highly compensated Solutions Engineer making $100,000+ a year. I was 29 years old, newly married, and extremely comfortable. I had a wonderful job but realized the path to BIG money and reaching a corporate officer position was through the <u>sales</u> organization.

I accepted a $60,000 pay cut and took a leap of faith into outside sales. I believed if I worked hard and listened to my Sales Manager, I would close numerous sales, make tons of money, and earn a quick promotion. To my surprise, I was not given a defined sales territory, any formal sales training, nor any existing clients. To make things even more difficult, my sales manager provided little direction or training. I had no idea what I was doing and spent my first year running in circles, stumbling through the sales process, and learning on the go. It was the worst experience in my professional career and pushed me to the brink of disaster.

Through trial and error, I created the **Blue Print**. This defined sales process helped me penetrate many new clients and build a lucrative account base from scratch, which billed over $4 million of revenue for Sprint in less than 3 years. I became one of Sprint's best sales professionals and this systematic process was the catalyst to my success. The victorious strategies outlined in my **Blue Print** can be applied to any industry. If you faithfully execute my **Blue Print** on a daily basis, money, recognition, and career progression will follow you!

Chapter 2
What is the **Blue Print**?

"If given six hours to chop down a tree,
I would spend the 1st five hours sharpening my axe."

- Abraham Lincoln, 16th President of the United States -

The **Blue Print** is a combination of strategic, creative, and consistent methods to penetrate new markets, expand and strengthen existing customer relationships, and close more sales. Bottom line, this game plan will help you **MAKE MORE MONEY**!!!!!!

The **Blue Print** will teach you the following essential skills:

- Clever ways to land appointments

- Improve your telemarketing skills — *better execution of the infamous "cold call"*

- Effectively manage the entire sales cycle — *from first appointment to closing the sale*

- Build a Contact Plan — *an organized process to penetrate new prospects*

- Successful execution of the "**DRIVE-BY**" — *most effective way to land an appointment with a new client*

- Embrace the explosion of social networking tools

- Capture the force of the "**Written**" Thank You card

- Leverage the power of the Administrative Assistant (AA)

- Improve your Questioning and Closing skills

- **ASK FOR THE BUSINESS**

- Build long-term relationships with your clients that lead to referrals and repeat business

- Do the simple things (Sales 101) — *professional follow up after formal meetings, reading on a regular basis, preparing for customer appointments, etc.*

- Utilize business tools to manage your daily sales activity

- Cultivate a strong professional network

- Find mentors

- Gain visibility within your organization

- **STAY POSITIVE** during tough times

If you follow the specific tactics outlined in the **Blue Print**, you will see immediate progress that will impact your sales results. I performed all aspects of my **Blue Print** in direct sales and used this strategic process to build the top sales team at Sprint. I am currently leveraging my **Blue Print** to lead one of the top performing areas at Sprint as a Regional Sales Director.

THE BLUE PRINT IS A PROVEN FORMULA THAT WILL PRODUCE RESULTS!!!!

In order to understand the **Blue Print**, you must embrace the following fundamental concept before reading another page:

— *Very Simple Formula* —

The More **HOURS** You Put In = The More **PROSPECTS** You Find

The More **PROSPECTS** You Find = The More **CALLS** You Make

The More **CALLS** You Make = The More **APPOINTMENTS** You Get

The More **APPOINTMENTS** You Get = The More **PROPOSALS** You Develop

The More **PROPOSALS** You Develop = The More **SALES** You Make

The More **SALES** You Make = The More **$$$$$** You Make

The More **$$$$$** You Make = *Higher Quality of Life You Provide Your Family*

Through trial and error, I discovered that one single method was not enough to penetrate a new client and start a meaningful business relationship. The **Blue Print** will teach you an organized process with multiple contact methods, to gain a first appointment, manage the sales process, close the sale, and build a long-term relationship with your clients. It will also teach you the basic lessons of professional sales that

95% of sales professionals no longer perform, such as a simple meeting follow up, written thank you notes, and leveraging the power of the administrative assistant. The **Blue Print** will clearly differentiate you from the other sales professionals in your respective industry and give you a competitive advantage to close more deals!

Chapter 3
Why Sales?
Are You Sure You Want To Do This?

- The Essence of Survival -

Every morning in Africa, a gazelle wakes up.
It knows it must run faster than the fastest lion or it will be killed.
Every morning a lion wakes up.
It knows it must outrun the slowest gazelle or it will starve to death.
It doesn't matter whether you are a lion or a gazelle,
when the sun comes up, you better be running.

- African Proverb -

Professional sales is a very tough career choice. On a daily basis, you are faced with rejection, pressure to deliver results, and adversity. This profession can be very lucrative but you must be willing to work hard or you will NOT make any money!

Everything starts with a sale! An elite sales professional is the life blood of any prosperous company. Without an aggressive sales force, all the other organizations cease to exist (*i.e. marketing, finance, human resources, operations, information technology, legal, senior leadership, etc.*). In most companies, the top sales reps easily make $100,000+ incomes and are usually the most valuable employees. Also, most senior executives in large corporations are former sales reps or spent time in the sales organization.

With that said, professional sales is **NOT** for everyone. Next to professional sports, it is the most competitive profession in business. It is intense, results driven, and clearly embodies the following concept — *survival of the fittest*. If you do not perform on a consistent basis, it is highly likely you will lose your job.

In order to dominate this tough profession, you must be competitive, driven, and highly motivated by money, recognition, and success. You must also clearly understand your "**WHY**," which are the key factors driving your quest for success. Your motivation could be putting your kids through college, buying a new house, paying off student loans, maintaining an extravagant lifestyle, putting food on the table for your family, advancing your career, etc. Without an intimate connection with your "**WHY**," one can easily succumb to the negative pressures surrounding this arduous profession that cause many to lose faith when times are tough.

Over the past nine years, I have had the pleasure to hire and support many elite sales professionals. Their personalities are vastly unique; however, the core characteristics that define how they approach the art of sales are almost identical. Here are the twelve consistent traits that define a successful sales professional — *fearless, passionate, persistent, hard working, organized, energetic, positive attitude, creative, competitive, willing to embrace constant knowledge development, and possession of the "IT" Factor, which is the unique ability to generate interest with strangers.* These characteristics are consistent across all winning sales professionals, regardless of industry.

On the flip side, there are specific traits that cause people to fail in this tough profession. *Fear of rejection, lack of organization, lack of creativity, and the inability to sacrifice and put in the grunt work* are the four simple characteristics that define why people fail in professional sales. These four characteristics are also consistent across all under-performing sales professionals, regardless of industry.

Back to the discussion on understanding your <u>WHY</u>. This is an extremely important topic because your <u>WHY</u> is the burning desire within your heart to succeed despite the obstacles and challenges you encounter each day. Your <u>WHY</u> is your true motivation.

> *"We all dream for something bigger; something bigger than this miniscule life we're leading. But where do we draw the line? How do we decide what is good enough, and how do we decide if we should dream bigger?"*

> *- Unknown Author -*

In order to really understand your "<u>WHY</u>," you must know the answers to the following meaningful questions:

What motivates me?

Am I competitive?

Do I HATE losing?

Can I deal with constant rejection?

Can I deal with constant pressure?

Am I comfortable with having my salary directly tied to my results?

Am I willing to dedicate 50+ hours every week to become a top performer?

Am I willing to work on the weekends to prepare myself for the up-coming week?

Am I comfortable talking with complete strangers?

What are my financial goals?

If the responses below describe you, then jump into professional sales **IMMEDIATELY** because the perilous obstacles that you will endure will not impact your spirit and determination to succeed:

What motivates me? — *Money, recognition, providing a higher standard of living for my family, success, winning, being #1, and competition!*

Am I competitive? — *Absolutely! I love to compete, win, and dominate.*

Do I HATE losing? — *YES! I hate losing more than winning. It really bothers me to lose to my competition. When I taste defeat, I put in more hours to ensure I do not lose again!*

Can I deal with constant rejection? — *Yes, the more times I hear the word NO, the more opportunities to hear the word YES...Rejection means the client did not understand my product. The word "No" means "Yes," just not right now.*

Can I deal with constant pressure? — *Yes, I love challenge! I have hobbies and a personal life to relieve stress and pressure. I have balance in my life and leave the pressure at work.*

Am I comfortable with having my salary directly tied to my results? — *Yes, I want the opportunity to over-achieve and be compensated for my hard work.*

Am I willing to dedicate 50+ hours every week to become a top performer? — *Yes, I will do whatever it takes to be #1. I am not afraid of hard work.*

Am I willing to work on the weekends to prepare myself for the up-coming week? — *Yes, I firmly believe that the battle is won before it is ever fought. I am willing to sacrifice personal time to ensure my success.*

Am I comfortable talking with complete strangers? — *I LOVE meeting new people!*

What are your financial goals? — *Six figures or more!*

If the following responses below describe you, I strongly recommend a different career path as the challenges of professional sales will crush your spirit:

What motivates me? — *I am not motivated by money or recognition. I do NOT like to compete on a regular basis. Winning isn't that significant to me.*

Am I competitive? — *Not really. I would rather not be forced to compete all of the time.*

Do HATE losing? — *I don't like to lose but sometimes it is OK to lose. We can't win all of the time...*

Can I deal with constant rejection? — *I HATE rejection and take it personal. It makes me feel bad and hurts my feelings.*

Can I deal with constant pressure? — *NO, I do not like pressure or being under lots of stress. Also, I don't like change.*

Am I comfortable with having my salary directly tied to my results? — *No. I am not a risk taker. I prefer a fixed salary that is guaranteed.*

Am I willing to dedicate 50+ hours every week to become a top performer? — *No. My personal time outside of my 40 hour work week is too important to me.*

Am I willing to work on the weekends to prepare myself for the up-coming week? — *No. My weekends are my personal time. I am only willing to work Monday through Friday.*

Am I comfortable talking with complete strangers? — *I am not comfortable talking with strangers or meeting new people. I prefer to be around people I know.*

What are your financial goals? — *I just want enough money to pay my bills and live a comfortable life.*

In conclusion, sales is NOT for everyone! It is a glamorous career path that provides an outstanding way to earn money but it also comes with daily challenges. Once you define and clearly understand your true motivation, you will know in your heart if sales is the right career choice. If you are prepared to deal with the trials & tribulations presented by this tough profession, you have made the right choice! Stay closely connected to your **WHY** and you will easily walk through any obstacles that may impede your pathway to success!

*"No matter where you are from,
we all dream of something better."*

- Anonymous -

Why I Selected Professional Sales
My Personal Story

Growing up, I did not realize professional sales would be my chosen career path. I aspired to be successful, make a great deal of money, and control my own destiny but a career in sales was never at the top of my list. I wanted to select a profession that was well respected and lucrative so I figured Medicine was the way to go.

During my freshman year at Morehouse College in Atlanta, Georgia, I decided to major in biology (pre-med). I did extremely well my freshman year and was selected to participate in a highly prestigious bio-medical research internship at Yale Medical School. The great thing about being selected to this esteemed program was that all of the participants had an inside track to attend Yale Medical School after graduation.

That summer, I interned with a renowned cardiovascular heart surgeon at Yale Medical School. This gentleman was recognized as one of the top heart surgeons in the US and I was learning from the best! During the summer, I quickly realized that I did not enjoy being in the hospital, going on rounds to see patients, and conducting lab research. Even though I felt the warning signs that medicine was not for me, I was mesmerized by the prestige of Yale, an elite Ivy League school that promised money and prominence, as well as the earning potential of being a heart surgeon. The last day of the internship, my doctor took me to witness a "live" open-heart surgery. During the surgery, I threw up and had to be carried out of the operating room! I quickly realized that I could not stomach the gory part of the human anatomy and there was **NO** way I could be a doctor.

When I returned to Morehouse for my sophomore year, I immediately switched my major to Political Science. This time around, I decided the legal profession was a quick way to fortune and prominence minus the blood and the need to operate on the human anatomy. I excelled in Political Science and was selected to an internship at the State Bar of

Georgia. During that particular summer, I quickly realized the legal profession was not a glitzy position where I would be delivering eloquent
speeches in court, wearing fancy suits, entertaining clients at 5-star res-
taurants, and leaving work at 4 PM in my convertible Porsche. Instead, I
would be cooped up in an office reviewing documents and meeting with
other lawyers to negotiate settlements. This honorable profession was
not for me, despite its importance to society and the opportunity to
make lots of money.

I was going into my third year of college with no clear direction. To complicate matters, my parents had just paid for my older brother to attend
MIT (Massachusetts Institute of Technology), which was an extremely
expensive school, and I had a younger sister heading for college right
after me. My parents were not rich and I knew I had to graduate in
four years.

I was fortunate to be blessed with athletic talent. I earned a football
scholarship to Morehouse College and evolved into an exceptional
player. I played outside linebacker and was a four year starter. Outside of
missing a few games due to injury, I started every game throughout my
college career. In my heart, I truly believed I had the talent to play professional football in the NFL (National Football League). I knew that if I
did not make an attempt to go pro, I would regret this decision throughout my life. Since Morehouse College was a Division II school, I knew my
path to the NFL was through Canada. I spent the winter and spring of
my senior year of college training extremely hard in preparation for the
upcoming tryouts to the Canadian Football League (CFL).

I excelled in the tryouts and was fortunate enough to be invited to training camp. Out of 350 players, the team only had 37 roster spots. I performed extremely well in a grueling and ultra competitive training camp
and made the team. I was officially a professional football player in the
CFL! This was an awesome experience; however, I quickly realized that
I would not make my mark in the world playing professional football.
After playing a full season in Canada, I ended my stint as a professional
football player and returned to Atlanta to find a job. My plan was to work
for 1 year (*save money and study for the GMAT*), attend graduate school,
and figure out my next step. I started working at Sprint and knew immediately that telecommunications was the industry where I could accomplish my dreams.

Sprint is the only company I have ever worked for since graduating
Cum Laude from Morehouse College with a degree in Political Science. I
achieved success in customer service, network operations, project management, and engineering during the first part of my career at Sprint.
However, it became evident that the path to BIG money and career

progression was through the sales organization. Most CEOs, business owners, and senior executives have spent time in sales. Since I have a burning passion to be a CEO one day, I took a **$60,000** pay cut, and jumped into sales!

PART 2
Blue Print Fundamentals

Chapter 4
Creating Your Value Statement

"By failing to prepare, you are preparing to fail."

- Benjamin Franklin, American Statesman, Scientist, & Philosopher -

All C-Level decision-makers and business owners are extremely busy people. It is very difficult to catch their attention so when that treasured chance presents itself, you must be concise, engaging, and relevant. You have less than thirty seconds to capture their interest before they tune you out, start multi-tasking, or completely cut you off!

Value statements are your unique opportunity to give someone a short commercial of who you are, what you do, and how you can help them! In order to hold someone's interest, you must be able to deliver a powerful Value Statement at all times.

Here is the definition of a Value Statement:

A short, concise, and relevant synopsis of who you are, what you do, and how the company you represent helps your clients achieve success.

There are five fundamentals in developing an outstanding value statement. It must be authentic, creative, clearly highlight your unique strengths, eloquently state why someone should trust you, and provide a compelling reason why someone should buy from you. The trick is you must be able to convey this material in a succinct fashion and make it interesting enough to entice people to crave more.

Once you determine the criteria to build your value statement, you must be able to articulate this information in three primary areas. Here are three critical value statements you must be able to deliver at **ALL** times:

1. **Why someone should do business with <u>YOUR</u> company?**

2. **Why someone should do business with <u>YOU</u>?**

3. **Be able to eloquently explain what <u>YOU</u> do for a living?**

Here is a perfect example of an outstanding value statement:

I help my clients leverage technology to make more money, secure a competitive advantage in their respective industry, better serve their customers, and gain more productivity from their employees. **How Do I Accomplish This?** *— Sprint has over 200 solutions that can be customized for business customers. I understand my client's goals/challenges and help them use our massive product portfolio to achieve success.*

This value statement is short, concise, and tells the potential client how you can help them. At the end of the day, you must communicate **"what's in it for them,"** in order to peak their interest for more.

DELIBERATE PRACTICE MAKES PERFECT! You must constantly practice and work on the delivery of your value statement so your words flow smoothly and sound natural. There are several ways you can practice to hone your delivery. The easiest way to hone your value statement is to see how you actually look and sound. I recommend that you practice in front of the mirror and evaluate your body language. Also, record yourself and listen to how your voice actually sounds. This maneuver will ensure your voice tone is generating excitement and interest.

Another excellent way to practice is to deliver your value statement to your significant other, friends, and family. This will ensure that the average person that may not be familiar with your industry finds you interesting. If I can explain the technology business to my father (*a retired Army Colonel who doesn't care about technology nor understand it*), then it will be very easy to deliver an alluring value statement to a C-Level or business owner who is probably not very proficient in technology nor really cares. All they care about is how can I help them accomplish their goals! Finally, practice your value statement in your weekly staff meeting amongst your peers. Stand up and deliver your value statement to your colleagues and solicit feedback. Of all people, they are proficient with your products and services and can provide constructive criticism to help improve your delivery. These exercises will make your delivery concise yet interesting!

In conclusion, you must be able to capture someone's interest in order to succeed in professional sales. Never forget that you are targeting busy people with vast levels of responsibility. These folks are being pulled in many different directions and have little time or patience. To make your job even more difficult, these individuals are probably complete strangers so you have less than thirty seconds to spark their interest. Therefore, you must be able to deliver a strong value statement at ALL times! If you master these three versions and practice on a consistent basis, you will have success captivating the interest of everyone you encounter!

Chapter 5
The Importance of Time Management Skills

"Time is the most valuable thing a man can spend."

- Theophrastus, Greek philosopher -

As a sales professional, **TIME** is your most important asset. Throughout the day, there are **REWARDS** and **CONSEQUENCES** for every decision you make. This chapter will review some best practices to stay organized and manage your time wisely.

Before we begin, we need to determine the monetary value of your time (*how much each hour of your time is worth throughout the business day*). We will use a very simple formula to calculate this critical metric. Here are the fundamentals to this recipe:

- **PRIME SELLING TIME** is between 8 AM — 5 PM

- **8 Hours** of critical selling time in each day — *subtract 1 hour for lunch, breaks, etc.*

- **40 Hours** of critical selling time in each week

- **52 Total Weeks** in each calendar year

- **2,080 Total Hours** of SELLING TIME in the year — (40 hours X 52 Weeks = 2,080)

- Based on a financial goal of **$200,000**, every hour of the day is worth **$96.15**. Here is a snap shot of the formula to calculate the value of each hour:

- **Formula** — *40 hours x 52 weeks = 2,080*

- **Formula** — *$200,000/2,080 = $96.15*

- **Caveat** — *If your financial goal is higher, simply change the yearly salary figure.*

» **Special <u>Blue Print</u> Tip** — *If for some reason, your financial goal is lower than **$100,000** per year, GET OUT OF PROFESSIONAL SALES IMMEDIATELY!!! Your goal should be a minimum of six figures!*

Before we go any further, you must embrace an extremely significant **<u>Blue Print</u>** fundamental regarding time management. I strongly encourage you to execute this important concept:

<u>**Never go to lunch with co-workers**</u> — *unless they can buy from you or you can learn from them!*

Many times, I see groups of sales professionals going to lunch together. I can fathom this decision on a sunny Friday afternoon once per quarter to catch up but I cannot understand why a group of sales reps would do this numerous times throughout the week. This will NOT lead to a new sale or help you make money! If you are going to have lunch during the week, meet with a prospect that may become a future client, existing customer for relationship building purposes, or a business partner to exchange leads. Your co-workers CANNOT buy anything from you; therefore, I strongly advise you to reserve your weekends for social time and preserve the precious weekdays for selling!

To put things in perspective, ask yourself the following question — **Are you willing to pay a co-worker (someone who can't buy from you) $96.15 to join you for lunch?**

I seriously doubt you would answer yes to this question. If so, please put yourself out of your own misery and find another way to earn income!

Now that you understand the value of each hour, I would like to cover some main priorities. A great method to properly manage your time during the day is to constantly ask yourself the following question:

Is This Activity Going To Help Me Make Money and Close Business?

If the answer is **<u>NO</u>**, then I strongly recommend that you do not perform this task or activity during normal business hours.

When making decisions on how to allocate your time, it is crucial to have a methodology to prioritize your activities. This methodology will give you the ability to make quick decisions and focus on the right things during prime time which is 8 AM — 5 PM!

Here are the **<u>SIX</u>** fundamental priorities for a sales professional: (**#1**) — daily prospecting (*activities focused on generating new business opportunities*), (**#2**) — working to close existing opportunities (*focusing your efforts* *on closing all pending deals in your sales funnel)*, (**#3**) — taking care of your existing customer base which leads to repeat business and referrals, (**#4**) — networking to cultivate your professional network of business contacts, (**#5**) — professional and personal development (*reading, product training, practicing your value statements, attending professional seminars, meeting with your mentors, etc.*), (**#6**) — working on administrative duties and non-service impacting support issues (*make sure you conduct these activities after hours such as expense reports, non-service impacting billing issues, sales reports, etc.*)

If you stack rank your daily activities based on this priority list, you will maximize your time throughout the day! I will now cover some excellent tips to stay organized.

First, commit to making a daily "**To-Do**" list. This best practice consists of creating a fresh priority list every day of hot items that require action. On this "**To-Do**" list, you need to number each item based on priority and use this list to govern how you allocate your time throughout the work day.

Here is a great example of a daily priority list:

#1 — prospecting for new business (make 50 cold-calls)

#2 — place a follow up call with Company A on the outstanding sales proposal I presented last week

#3 — produce a new sales proposal to formally present to Company B tomorrow

#4 — send follow up emails for the 15 drive-bys that I conducted yesterday

#5 — summarize the action items from the customer meeting I had yesterday and send a formal MOU (*memo of understand — short email that documents the action items from the meeting and is sent to the client within 24 to 48 hours after the appointment*) to the client

#6 — prepare for my 1st appointment with Company C tomorrow

#7 — send follow up emails to the 50 cold calls that I made yesterday

#8 — escalate the resolution of the outstanding billing issues for Companies D, E, & F,

#9 — complete my expense report

As you finish each action item, reward yourself by scratching completed items off your list (*it is a refreshing feeling at the end of the day to see your "to-do" list with several items completed*). This process will also allow you to determine how productive your day was especially if you were able to finish many of the action items. If you failed to complete many of your high priority items, then put in more hours or work on your time management skills! As you can see from this list, the sales professional with this much activity must put in more than 8 hours per day in order to complete these hot items which will lead to BIG money!

Second, put **ALL** customer appointments, strategy sessions, and meetings on your calendar. This process will keep you organized and ensure you never miss an important meeting.

Third, create a library/filing system within your email account. For example, I create personal folders for all areas critical to my business and file pertinent material into these folders. This is a resourceful system to quickly find data when you need it. It also allows you to instantly locate critical files or historical notes (*proposals, pricing quotes, contracts, etc.*) when you need them in tight situations. Finally, this system gives you the opportunity to re-use and enhance previous documents and eliminate the need to start from scratch. Remember — time is money so being able to embellish previous works will save time and increase productivity which leads to more money in your bank account.

Fourth, I strongly encourage you to invest in a CRM (Customer Relationship Management) tool. I religiously use Salesforce.com to manage all of my customer contact information, sales opportunities, 30/60/90 day sales funnel, appointment activity, sales proposals, etc. We will cover this topic in greater detail in the up-coming chapter entitled "Powerful Business Tools to Manage your Sales Activity."

Fifth, constantly ask yourself the following question throughout the day — "*Is this activity going to help me make MONEY or get me closer to winning the next deal?*" If the answer is no, **DON'T DO THIS DURING PRIME SELLING HOURS**! We covered this topic earlier in this chapter; however, I feel compelled to remind you of this critical point.

Sixth, empower yourself to delegate the appropriate workload to the internal resources that support your sales efforts. Many times, I see sales professionals trying to do **EVERYTHING** by themselves and not relying on the experts that are paid to support them. These are very talented individuals with tremendous expertise. Let them help you! Also, please hold them accountable to doing their job. Do not allow them to dump their responsibilities on your plate. Remember our discussion on how much every hour of your day is worth? If your financial goal is $200,000 per year, you are essentially paying an internal resource **$96.15** out of your own pocket to dump their responsibilities on your plate. Would you really write them a check for $96.15? I seriously doubt it. They receive a paycheck every two weeks regardless if you win deals or not so make them earn their salary. We (*the fearless sales professionals*) live and die on our commissions and bonuses. If we do not sell, we do not eat. Do not feel ashamed to hold these critical resources accountable for doing their job. Finally, if they do a fabulous job, make sure you say "Thank You" and treat them like gold! Many sales reps forget to thank the hard working resources that support their accounts. If you treat them with respect and remember to say thank you, they will work harder to support your efforts. Being nice and saying "thank you" goes a long way!

Seventh, act like a Chief Executive Officer (CEO)! Whether you work for a fortune 100 company or small business, you are truly running your own company. We are all independent contractors that happen to receive a pay check from a larger entity. The companies we work for merely provide us with training, resources, and support. It is our responsibility to generate new business opportunities, manage existing client relationships, and close deals. Always remember that you are running your own business so you must approach each day with the attitude and focus of a CEO.

Last but most critical, you must set <u>ONE</u> new appointment <u>EVERY</u> day! New business development is the life blood to your success. If you can set a new appointment each and every day, you will always make quota and maintain a robust sales funnel!

> » **Special <u>Blue Print</u> Tip** — *In addition to making a daily "To-Do" list, I also encourage you to keep a daily **NOT** "To-Do" list. There are several items you should NOT do during prime selling time, such as administrative tasks, non-service impacting customer service work that could probably wait until after hours, going to lunch with co-workers, etc. Keep this list handy and if you find yourself doing items from the NOT list, stop immediately. Remember to constantly ask yourself this meaningful question throughout the day — **"Is this activity going to help me get closer to winning a sale?"** If the answer is no, don't conduct this activity between the hours of 8 AM — 5 PM.*

In conclusion, time is the most important asset you have. There are only **2,080** total hours of selling time in each calendar year. You must stay organized, manage your time wisely, and keep the precious hours of **8 AM — 5 PM** focused strictly on sales activity! Remember to always ask yourself the following question — *"Is this activity going to help me close a sale or make money?"* If the answer is *"this activity will **NOT** help me close a sale,"* STOP IMMEDIATELY and focus on activities that will lead to new business! As a sales professional operating a personal enterprise, time is definitely money!

Chapter 6
Leveraging the Power of
Written Communication

"The most valuable of all talents is that of never using __two__ words when __one__ will do."

- Thomas Jefferson, 3rd President of the United States -

Email has become the primary method of communication in today's business culture. On average, business owners and C-Level decision-makers receive 300 or more emails per day. These folks are extremely busy people. It is extremely difficult to catch their attention so you must be concise, engaging, and relevant. They will probably only read the first few sentences of your message before losing interest. The longer your message, the higher likelihood it will be deleted or ignored.

EVERYONE HATES LONG EMAILS! Think about your own reaction to a lengthy email that hits your in-box. Personally, I cringe when I see these drawn-out messages. They are very hard to digest and easy to delete.

To put things in perspective, it is very essential to understand the mind-set of a busy individual with significant responsibility. Here is the methodology I use to prioritize and respond to emails — (**#1**) — my wife (*my children fall into this category; however, they are only 6 & 4 years old and not ready to send emails just yet*), (**#2**) — my customers, (**#3**) — my direct-reports, (**#4**) — my boss which includes my senior leadership team, (**#5**) — my peers and internal business colleagues, (**#6**) — sales professionals attempting to pitch their product to me, and (**#7**) — strangers.

As you can see from this stack rank, sales professionals have one of the lowest priorities on this list. I have no choice but to tolerate a lengthy message from one through five; however, I will delete or ignore a long message from sales professionals or strangers. There are not enough hours in the day to review long emails from folks in the last two categories. This is exactly the mind-set of the business owners and C-level decision-makers you are trying to reach.

Going forward, you must ingrain the following phrase into your mind when drafting emails — **SHORTER IS ALWAYS BETTER!** With that said, there are five ways to ensure your written communication is not ignored. **First**, keep all written communication short, relevant, and concise. **Second**, do not write emails longer than three paragraphs when communicating to external clients. **Third**, do not use more than three sentences per paragraph. **Fourth**, do not use huge or multi-color font in your emails. I strongly recommend Times New Roman or Arial with a font size of "11," "10.5," or "10". **Last but most important,** always proof read your content for errors. The quickest way to ensure your email will be deleted is to have spelling or grammatical errors. An email riddled with blunders sends the wrong message and could be interpreted that you are unprofessional or not very smart. Please arrange your email account to automatically check ALL outgoing messages for errors using "spell check". Spell check will help you send articulate emails that will make a positive impression on your customers and potential clients!

When you are attempting to schedule appointments, always provide three dates and times when asking for a meeting (*always one to two weeks out*). Here is a brilliant example of a method to land an appointment with a decision-maker (*this meeting request is based on the assumption that your email was sent the week of 12-5-2011*):

Please let me know what date and time is most convenient:

- *Wednesday-Dec. 14th — Anytime after 12 PM*

- *Thursday-Dec. 15th — Anytime before 1 PM*

- *Tuesday-Dec. 20th — morning & afternoon are currently open*

Thank you in advance and I look forward to hearing back from you.

This tactic will help you land more appointments. When you frame your request in this format, you are providing a busy and important decision-maker several opportunities to meet with you. Quite often, senior executives and business owners are booked several weeks in advance for meetings. By asking for a meeting one to two weeks out, you increase the probability your client will be available. Finally, you directly asked for a specific response. Now, the prospect must respond with either YES or NO instead of blowing you off.

In summary, keep all written correspondence short, succinct, and relevant. **EVERYONE HATES LONG EMAILS**! In today's society, everyone is juggling numerous obligations that range from business to family life. Unfortunately, there just are not enough hours in the day! Given this reality, business owners and C-level decision-makers cannot respond to every email that hits their in-box. If you are brief and straight to the point, you increase the probability that your written correspondence will capture their attention!

Chapter 7
Master your Questioning Skills

"Questioning is the door of knowledge."

- Irish Saying -

Growing up, I was fascinated by murder mysteries and detective shows like Perry Mason, Murder She Wrote, and Remington Steele (*starring the silky smooth detective played by Pierce Brosnan*). Today, I rarely watch TV but always make time to watch CSI Miami (*Lieutenant Horatio Caine played by David Caruso is the coolest detective on TV*). One of my all time favorites is Law & Order: Criminal Intent featuring the eccentric detective Robert Goren played by Vincent D'Onofrio. When my daughter was born, my wife and I were cooped up in the hospital a few extra days as she recovered from a c-section. During our stay, we ended up watching a Law & Order: Criminal Intent marathon on the USA network which featured every single episode staring Vincent D'Onofrio. I grew very fond of the awesome questioning skills and interrogation tactics detective Goren used to solve intricate cases and force diabolical suspects to confess to horrendous crimes. His character is a great listener with the innate ability to connect with people across all walks of life.

In each episode of CSI Miami and Law & Order, the detectives are responsible for solving puzzling homicides committed by calculated killers. These investigators rely on a combination of instincts, questioning skills, and technology. They arrive to the scene of the crime and are tasked with discovering what happened, who did it, and why. Through excellent questioning skills and analyzing evidence, they identify the perpetrator and uncover their motive for committing these horrific crimes. At the end of each show, they force the suspect into a dramatic confession using their powerful interrogation skills.

I can easily correlate the questioning skills of an exceptional homicide detective/CSI investigator to those of an elite sales professional. The mark of all winning sales professionals is the ability to ask brilliant questions. Honing this craft is essential to dominating your respective industry. Similar to a homicide detective attempting to solve a perplexing crime, this specialized skill will uncover the essential information to help your client accomplish their goals using your product/service. At the end of the day, this leads to large commission check and BIG MONEY in your bank account!

People (*especially business owners and C-Level executives*) love to talk about themselves, their accomplishments, and their business problems. They have dedicated their lives to building and running a successful business. Because of their passion to excel, they are always willing to share this material with anyone that shows sincere interest. The more you learn about what makes them tick, the better positioned you will be to help them accomplish their goals. Also, the more you learn about their company, the easier it will be for you to position your products and services to close more sales! If they believe you are genuinely interested in the well-being of their business, they will open up and share vital data. Once you become their trusted advisor, it will be extremely easy to sell your products and services. This can only be accomplished via surgical questioning skills.

Before you begin asking questions, you must know your audience and what drives their thought process. Each level within the chain of command has different priorities and interests. It is critical to understand how these folks think in order to ask the right questions. One significant point to remember is the higher you climb the chain of command, the more strategic-minded the individuals will be. On the reverse, the lower you travel down the chain of command, the more tactical-minded the person is.

Here is a complete breakdown of the priorities and thought processes within the various levels of the chain of command:

The CEO / President / Principal / Owner

This leader is the most strategic minded person in business. They are responsible for devising and executing the long term vision, controlling the company's public perception, and understanding key trends within their industry that will impact the long-term growth of their company. They are mainly interested in overall financial health of the company (*top line revenue, the bottom line/net income, and losses after expenses*). The top dog is also responsible for communicating the company's vision, performance, and strategic direction to Wall Street, shareholders, potential investors, and the general public. Finally, they are very interested in ways to increase market share, motivate their employees, gain a competitive advantage, and retain their existing base of customers.

Here are some compelling questions to ask the CEO/President:

- What are your company's long term strategic goals?

- What are the most significant growth areas for your company over the next 3 years?

- What are the biggest challenges your company faces over the next 3 — 5 years (*what keeps you up at night*)?

- How do you inspire your employees to meet these challenges?

- How does your company separate itself from the competition?

- What initiatives have you considered to increase sales and grow market share?

- How does your board measure your success?

- How is your company navigating through this challenging economic environment?

- Do you have any important changes you would like to implement to improve your company's overall operations?

- If you could instantly change any aspect of business, what would it be?

- What would happen to your company if you could implement those changes?

The CFO / VP Finance of Sales / Financial Departments

In the past, the CFO was considered a bean counter responsible for protecting the company's cash. Over the past 20 years, this role vastly changed due to the wave of corporate scandals (*remember Enron, WorldCom, and Tyco*) and the pressure on companies to deliver positive financial results every quarter. The CFO now holds a wide variety of important roles such as general managerial responsibilities, financial expertise, representing the company to the finance community, helping to negotiate complex mergers/acquisitions, and ensuring the company adheres to strict accounting regulations.

The CFO of today is interested in managing growth while controlling costs, increasing profitability, managing the company's balance sheet, and ensuring that all investments or expenditures have a solid return on investments (ROI). They are also responsible for insuring that more revenue comes in than expenses going out. Finally, the CFO is tasked with identifying acquisition opportunities for their respective company.

Here are some excellent questions to ask:

- What are the company's plans for growth over the next 3 — 5 years?

- How do you plan to manage costs as your organization grows?

- What are your initiatives to improve cash flow and increase the profitability of your company?

- What criteria do you use to evaluate an ROI and determine where to invest resources and money?

- What role does the CFO play in relation to the senior management team?

- What role does the CFO play in relation to the decision-making process?

- What are the biggest challenges your company faces over the next 3 — 5 years (*what keeps you up at night*)?

- How does your boss measure your success?

- How does your company separate itself from the competition?

- How is your company navigating through this challenging economic environment?

COO / CSO / VP Operations / VP Distribution / VP Supply Chain / Warehouse Manager

This executive is responsible for the day-to-day operations at the company. Streamlining operations, gaining more productivity from their employees, improving customer service, and the delivery time of their product or service is what drives their decisions.

Here are some great questions to ask:

- How do your front line employees interact and communicate with your customers?

- How do your sales people stay connected with their account base while in the field?

- How can your teams improve interaction with the tools and departments they rely on for support?

- How do you measure customer satisfaction?

- What are the biggest challenges your company faces over the next 3 — 5 years (*what keeps you up at night*)?

- How does your boss measure your success?

- How does your company separate itself from the competition?

- How is your company navigating through this challenging economic environment?

CIO / Director of IT / Director of Telecom

The Chief Information Officer (CIO) is the top information technology (IT) leader in a company. This person is usually the final decision-maker for technology decisions and primarily responsible for ensuring the company's IT strategy is directly tied to supporting the company's long term strategic goals.

Their main responsibilities are helping the company leverage technology as a competitive advantage, ensuring the IT infrastructure can support the end-users within the company, and staying current on technology trends and advancements. They are also concerned with ensuring that the company's help desk operations can support their external customers and all end users within the company. Finally, they are tasked with improving their Customer Relations Management tools (CRM), streamlining operations, and implementing a disaster recovery plan to manage natural disasters and emergencies.

Here are some solid questions to ask these decision-makers:

- What is the overall role of the CIO at your company?

- Does your company view technology as a strategic advantage or more of a necessary evil to conduct business?

- How does your company use technology to gain a competitive advantage?

- How does IT improve business operations, growth, and innovation?

- How do you evaluate your organization's overall performance and value to the business?

- How does your IT staff evaluate and determine the needs of the different business units you support?

- How do you link your IT strategy directly to the strategic direction of the company?

- What criteria is used to evaluate and guarantee that all IT investments deliver an ROI?

- What criteria do you use to evaluate the performance of vendors and business partners?

- What critical factors do you consider when planning an enterprise deployment?

- What key technology projects are you deploying over the next 24 months?

- How do you stay current with the technology trends impacting your industry?

- What are the biggest challenges your company faces over the next 3 — 5 years (*what keeps you up at night*)?

- How does your boss measure your success?

- How does your company separate itself from the competition?

- How is your company navigating through this challenging economic environment?

VP Sales / VP Marketing / Director of Sales / Director of Business Development

This executive is responsible for growing the company's overall market share, acquiring new clients, and retaining/growing their existing base of customers. This individual is primarily focused on increasing market share, maximizing revenues through deeper penetration of existing accounts, acquisition of new clients, and ensuring customer retention. They are also focused on improving the accuracy of sales forecasts, increasing the efficiency and productivity of their sales force, and training the sales force to be more knowledgeable. Finally, this executive is tasked with recruiting new sales talent and helping to launch and market new products/services.

Here are some awesome questions to ask this decision-maker:

- How does your company separate itself from the competition?

- How do you create customer loyalty?

- What is keeping your sales force from performing at the highest possible level?

- How does your company market your products/services?

- How is your company navigating through this challenging economic environment?

- How does your company recruit new sales talent?

- How does your team currently forecast sales?

- What have you done in the past to improve forecasting accuracy?

- What is your strategy to further penetrate existing accounts and acquire new clients?

- What tools and systems does your sales force utilize to conduct business?

- How does your sales force maintain customer relationships?

- How does your boss measure your success?

- What are the biggest challenges your company faces over the next 3 — 5 years (*what keeps you up at night*)?

  » **Special Blue Print Tip** — *Asking the following question provides several benefits — "How does your boss measure your success?" You will usually uncover much more than just the answer. The client will provide how they feel about their boss (usually non-verbal), insight into their personal goals, and knowledge about their fears. Finally, this question will help you understand how your solution can help make them successful. Once you have this critical data, you can clearly communicate how your solution will improve their success rating within their organization. This is a powerful way to become your client's trust advisor and ally. Making your client look like a hero is a very important skill set that all victorious sales professionals keep as their active focus! When they "win" using your solution, you win too!*

Now that you realize how each level within the chain of command thinks, it is essential to understand how to properly ask questions. One of the fundamentals to fabulous questioning skills is asking **OPEN-ENDED** questions. An open-ended question always starts with the following simple one-word phrases — **What, Where, When, How, Who**, and **Why**.

Beginning your questions with these open ended phrases will push your client to reveal the important data about their business operations and overall pain-points (*you need this information to properly position your solution*). Once you ask an open-ended question, pause, shut up, and **LISTEN.** They will give you all the information you need!

> » **Special <u>Blue Print</u> Tip** — *Powerful listening skills are one of the most important traits to becoming a winning sales professional. If you interviewed most top executives and business owners, they will tell you that many people are quiet when they are talking, but few truly listen for understanding. Many sales people are notoriously bad listeners in this respect. If you ask the right open-ended question and your client decides to fully engage and answer your question, you are receiving valuable data on their beliefs, priorities, core initiatives, etc. This information is extremely critical so shut up and listen. Don't think about what you're going to say next, pay attention, take notes, and fully comprehend the insight being bestowed upon you.*

NEVER ask leading questions, which are "<u>yes</u>" or "<u>no</u>" questions that basically suggest the answer. These types of questions give your client an easy way out and let them off the hook! When you ask a "leading" question, you are essential asking and answering the question for the client. These questions are very ineffective because you are basically "leading" your client to a certain response versus probing for new information.

Here are a few examples of leading questions (**the leading part is highlighted in BOLD**):

- What are your responsibilities at your company, **do you manage the sales organization**?

- Where is your corporate headquarters, **is it located in Dallas**?

- Who is your existing wireless vendor, **are you using AT&T**?

- When is your contract up with your existing vendor, **is it next year**?

- How do you handle shipping and logistics, **do you outsource this to another vendor or do you perform this task in-house**?

These are **CLOSE-ENDED** questions. If you phrase your questions in this format, you are letting them off way too easy. They can easily say **YES** or **NO** to these questions without elaborating.

Here is the best way to ask the same questions in an open-ended format:

- What are your responsibilities at your company?

- Where is your corporate HQ located?

- When is your contract up with your existing vendor?

- How do you handle logistics?

This line of questioning forces the client to elaborate. **Remember** — *decision-makers enjoy talking about their business.* If you demonstrate true interest, they will give you all of the material you need.

Here are the critical items you must uncover via surgical questioning:

- How your client makes money?

- What are their significant business challenges?

- What are their most important business objectives and priorities?

- What is your point of contact responsible for at their company?

- What are their long-term and strategic goals?

- How do they separate themselves from their competition?

- Who are their major competitors?

- What initiatives have they considered to increase sales, revenue, and customer satisfaction?

- What high priority projects are they focused on this fiscal or calendar year?

- What are their current challenges and biggest headaches (*day-to-day issues, pain-points, etc.*)?

- What primary changes would they like to implement to solve their business problems?

- How is their relationship being managed by the current vendor that sells your product/service (*are they happy, do they have a dedicated account team, are issues being resolved in a timely manner, how are they being supported, etc.*)?

- When does their contract expire with their existing vendor (*if they are currently under contract with another vendor that provides the service you are selling to this client*)?

- Who is the final decision-maker for your product/service at this company?

"He who asks a question is a fool for five minutes; he who does not ask a question remains a fool forever."
- Chinese Proverb -

The most fundamental questions in the sales process are **first appoint- ment questions** and **closing questions**. First appointment questions are extremely important because first impressions mean everything! The first appointment is your special opportunity to make a positive impression on your client and gather all of the essential data required to move your opportunity through the sales process. Closing questions are perhaps the most compelling because they result in winning the business and securing the contract. They will help uncover potential con- cerns that will delay your sale, identify the real decision-maker, flush out your competition, and identify the timeline when your client will place the order.

First appointment questions are categorized in the following sections — **Ice Breaker/Probing Questions** (*learn more about your client's busi- ness*), **Specific Product Questions** (*uncover their specific needs that help you position your product*), and **Company Specific Questions** (*educate the client on the power of your company*). Here are a few examples:

Ice Breaker — Probing Questions

- What are your responsibilities at your company?

- What are your company's strategic goals — ***I would like to confirm what I read on your web site*** (*please be prepared if the client tests your knowledge on what you actually know about their company*)?

- How does your company separate itself from the competition?

- What initiatives have you considered to increase Sales? Revenue? Customer Satisfaction?

- What are your most important projects this year?

- What are your current challenges and biggest headaches (*day-to- day issues, pain-points, etc.*)?

- How is your current relationship with your existing vendor (*are you happy, do you have a dedicated account team, how are you being supported, are issues being resolved in a timely manner*)?

Other questions can also probe for personal connections. Look for visual aids when you meet with your client. For example, you noticed a BMW in the CIO's parking spot, trophies from a local softball league, family pictures, memorabilia from their college alma mater, artwork, vacation photos (*exotic destinations you may have visited as well that could be used to spark a meaningful conversation*), etc. Use these clues to enhance your conversation and help establish a connection with your client.

Specific Product Questions

These are related to the wireless industry but can be altered to fit your specific industry.

- What kind of wireless applications are you using today?

- What kind of wireless applications do you plan to deploy in the future (*what would you like to implement; what is on your wish list*)?

- What are the needs of your mobile workers?

- What is the profile of your mobile workforce (*sales reps in the field, service technicians working jobs, consultants on site at customer locations, etc.*)?

- Does your company have any strategic initiatives to better equip your mobile workers to operate more efficiently?

- Is your company using any of the following technologies today — *machine-to-machine, mobile-resource-management, tablets, wireline convergence, mobile broadband technology, smartphones, etc.?*

Company Specific Questions

These questions will gauge how your client feels about the company you represent.

- What do you know about my company?

- Have you used my company's products in the past? If so, how was your experience?

- Have you heard about any of our exciting new product launches?

These surgical questions will help you uncover the necessary information to move the sales cycle in a positive direction, build credibility with your client, and uncover essential data to position your product.

> » **Special Blue Print Tip** — *An essential "ice-breaker" question to ask on every 1ˢᵗ appointment is the following — What are your responsibilities at your company? This question forces the client to tell you about their scope of responsibility. Many times, this question will open the door for the client to reveal their company structure, initiatives, and why they took the meeting. Also, the higher up the person is in the chain of command, the more material you will gather from asking this simple question. If the person has a vast amount of responsibility and decision-making authority,*

*they will **TELL YOU** and provide intricate details on the structure of the organization they lead! Remember, people with vast levels of responsibility are passionate about what they do and love sharing this information with anyone that shows sincere interest.*

Now that you know what questions to ask, let's briefly discuss the purpose of these questions. During the first appointment, you must gather the following critical information:

1. Learn how the prospect is currently using your type of product or service

2. Who is their current vendor?

3. What do they like and dislike about their current vendor?

4. When do their contracts expire?

5. Who is the decision-maker?

6. Who is involved in the decision-making process?

7. What is the decision-making process?

8. What is the timeline for making a final decision?

9. The person you are meeting with — *what are their roles/responsibilities at the company & have they had a previous experience working with your company?*

10. What are their most important business initiatives?

11. Do they have a legitimate need for your product or service?

12. How critical is your product or service to their business operations?

13. How do they view your company and have they used your company in the past?

Powerful Closing Questions

In order to close your sale, you must ask the pivotal questions below on **ALL** opportunities! Having these facts are critical to winning the deal. Without this important data, you are flying **BLIND.**

- What is the decision-making criteria for purchasing my product — *what 3 factors will you base your decision on?*

- Is this project **funded**? — *if you are selling a high dollar product/ service, it is critical that you discover if your client has the budget to afford your solution.*

- Can I help you build a Return on Investment (ROI) to justify the purchase of my solution?

- Who makes the final decision?

- What are the next steps in the process (*decision-making timeline*)?

- What other companies are you considering for this service (*this is a fancy way of asking who is my competition*)?

- What concerns do you have about moving forward with my company?

- What is the priority level of this project (*how urgent is the deployment of this solution*)?

- Since we identified how our proposed solution will impact your business operations in a positive way, what is the financial impact if you don't move forward (*if you have clearly identified significant pain points, this is a very strong question*)?

- What is the financial impact if our solution is not implemented by XX-X X-2012 (date)?

- What is the financial impact if you do not address the business challenges (*pain points*) we discussed in previous conversations?

- What is the financial impact if you don't make a change?

  » **Special <u>Blue Print</u> Tip** — *If your product requires the client to make a significant financial investment, it is important to determine if they have a budget to pay for your solution. If not, you must quickly determine if they will work directly with you to build a ROI (return of investment) to justify the purchase. If you cannot help them justify the expense, you need to move on to the next opportunity. Remember — TIME is your biggest asset! You cannot afford to pursue clients that do not have the budget to purchase your solution or the willingness to entertain an impressive ROI.*

In summary, honing your questioning skills is critical to dominating the field of professional sales! Just like a homicide detective attempting to solve a high profile crime, you must possess the ability to ask great questions in order to solve real business problems. Through powerful questioning skills, you will clearly understand your client's business challenges and always recommend the correct solution to help them succeed. If you can accomplish this task, you will definitely make **BIG MONEY** and separate yourself from the competition!

Chapter 8
The POWER of the "<u>Written</u>" Thank You Card

"Kindness is the language which the deaf can hear
and the blind can see."

- Mark Twain, Legendary Author -

Ninety-five percent of all sales professionals no longer leverage the power of the "**<u>written</u>**" thank you card. This maneuver will definitely separate you from your competition. In the client's eyes, it demonstrates that you really care about the prosperity of their business. It also illustrates kindness, respect, and thoughtfulness. I use this tactic frequently to run my business.

How do you feel when you receive a hand written thank you card from a family member, friend, or business colleague when they show gratitude for an act of kindness? On the flip side, how do you feel when someone does not show gratitude or say "thank you" when you go out of your way to help them? Recently, I loaned a close friend some money to start a business venture. It wasn't a great deal of money but it was meaningful enough to make a difference. A few weeks after my friend repaid me, I received a thank you card in the mail with a heartfelt note thanking me for my generosity. This small gesture warmed my heart and I truly felt their sincere appreciation. Imagine how your clients will feel when you add this weapon into your sales process!

> » **Special <u>Blue Print</u> Tip** — *ALWAYS send a hand written thank you card after ALL first sales to the final decision-maker and everyone within the company that helped you win the deal. Do NOT forget that many of your clients are making significant financial investments in your product or service. Many times, they are staking their career progression, reputation, and political power within their company to support your product. It adds an extra special touch when you send a hand written card to thank them for their business and their trust.*

Here are several occasions to exploit this graceful tool: (**#1**) — after your very first appointment with a new prospect, (**#2**) — after winning your first order or contract with a new client, (**#3**) — when an existing client sends you a referral, (**#4**) — when a receptionist or administrative assistant helps you land an appointment with the company's decision-maker (**#5**) — after a new prospect takes your telemarketing call but does not give you an appointment but you engage in meaningful conversation and they ask you to call back (*in this situation, sending a written thank you card will help build rapport and guarantee they remember you when you call back*), (**#6**) — after a formal interview for a job or internal promotion (*I personally eliminate all candidates that do not send a thank you card after a formal interview*).

> » **Special Blue Print Tip** — *In order to personalize your message and leave a lasting impression, always include a HAND WRITTEN NOTE in your thank you card. Try your best to make the note authentic but concise. Remember — shorter is always better!*

Here are four solid examples for hand written thank you notes. Also, always include your business card!

Example #1 — First Appointment

XXX,

*Thank you for your time on Thursday, January 5th. It was a pleasure learning more about your business operations and strategic goals. I am confident my company will be a valuable resource to XXX (**INSERT THE COMPANY NAME**) and help you gain a competitive advantage. I am very excited about the opportunity to earn your business and look forward to our next meeting.*

Sincerely,

Reggie Marable

Example #2 — Winning the Business

XXX,

Thank you so much for your business! I sincerely appreciate your trust in my ability to deliver impeccable service. You will be extremely happy with our solution and I am personally committed to ensuring you have a positive experience with my company. I look forward to developing a fruitful partnership. Once again, thank you for your business.

Sincerely,

Reggie Marable

Example #3 — Warm Referral

XXX,

*Thank you so much for the referral! I promise to give XXX (**INSERT THE COMPANY NAME**) special attention. Just like you, they will be pleased with my company's solution and I am personally committed to ensuring they have a positive experience. Once again, thank you for your referral.*

Sincerely,

Reggie Marable

Example #4 — Telemarketing Call

XXX,

*Thank you for taking my call on Thursday, January 5th. It was a pleasure learning more about your business operations and strategic goals. If given the opportunity to prove myself, I am confident my company will be a valuable resource to XXX (**INSERT COMPANY NAME**) and help you gain a competitive advantage. I'm very excited about the opportunity to earn your business and will give you another phone call on Monday, January 23rd to schedule a formal appointment. In the meantime, please call me at 404-555-5555 if there is anything I can do for you.*

Sincerely,

Reggie Marable

These are standard messages that I personally created and use on a consistent basis. The following web site has numerous examples to use for a variety of different occasions — www.thank-you-note-samples.com. This site is another great resource to reference for any occasion.

One of the largest deals I closed as a direct sales rep was because I used the power of the written thank you card. I was in an intense bidding process with my competition for a multi-million dollar contract. Since our proposed solution completely changed the way this company sold their product, we had to present our solution to their entire senior leadership team which included the CEO, COO, CIO, CFO, VP of Marketing, VP of Sales, and VP of HR. After our presentation, I made a point to secure business cards of everyone in attendance. Later that evening, I sent every executive a personal thank you card that included a hand written note. After we won the business, the CIO told me that one of the biggest reasons his company selected our solution was because of my "written" thank you cards. Here is a direct quote from the CIO:

*"Your product and price were similar to the other companies we considered. We chose to go with your company because you went above and beyond during the sales process to demonstrate that you really cared about our business. My CEO felt that if you took the time to write everyone on our leadership team a personal thank you note, we knew you would go the extra mile to ensure this project is a smashing success. You were the **ONLY** sales professional that demonstrated this level of passion during the sales process!"*

In summary, the power of sending written thank you cards will clearly separate you from the competition. This gesture demonstrates that you have genuine sincerity for your client's success, commitment to developing a lasting partnership, and respect for their time. Remember, at the end of the day, people buy from people they "**LIKE**" and "**TRUST**." Your clients are buying YOU along with your product. Written thank you cards will go a long way to demonstrate your passion and devout commitment to their prosperity!

Chapter 9
The Art of Generating Referral Business

*"Most people are content to let perfect days happen
at random rather than PLAN for them."*

- Unknown Author -

The **Blue Print** is a proven way to generate business the hard way (*cold calling, drive-bys, etc.*); however, the easiest way to generate new business opportunities is through warm referrals from your existing customer base. If you take care of your existing customers, they will refer business to you, if you simply ASK.

Think of your real estate agent, life insurance agent, and your financial advisor. These sales professionals live and die by referral business and have created a system to keep their pipeline full of awesome referrals. One of their keys to success is that they ASK you to personally refer them to your friends and business colleagues. I have personally referred at least 15 people to my financial advisor. Of these 15 or so referrals, he's successfully closed more than half, simply off of my warm introduction. Also, my hard working real estate agent has received several warm referrals that have led to new home sales. Because these assiduous sales professionals took care of my needs, I was happy to send them more business. Unfortunately, many outside sales professionals (*regardless of industry*) simply do not ask their existing customers for referrals and leave money on the table.

Here are six **Blue Print** fundamentals to land referral business from your existing customers:

Deliver on ALL Commitments

Your clients will measure your credibility based upon your actions. If you make a commitment, you must deliver. The quickest way to ruin a business relationship is failure to deliver on promises or commitments (*whether it is intentional or unintentional*). On the flip side, if you deliver on all commitments, you will gain your client's complete trust and they will believe in you. If you have their trust, they will refer their friends and colleagues to you. Remember, it is always better to under-promise and over-deliver!

Be Responsive

Whether your client contacts you by voice mail, email, or text message you must respond back within a reasonable time frame! Even if you cannot do so immediately or fully resolve their problem, at a minimum acknowledge their communication. A solid best practice is to say "*Hey April, I received your email. I am working on a solution to your billing issue and will have a status update within the next 3 business days.*" Now your client knows that you received their message and you are working to fix their problem. At the end of the day, all they want to know is that action is forthcoming to address their need. The worst thing you can do is not respond. If you are responsive to your client's needs, they will brag about this special trait with their colleagues and friends, which will translate into referrals for you!

> » **Special Blue Print Tip** — *Always respond to all emails and voice mails within 24 to 48 hours. In today's business environment, many sales professionals fall short in this area. If you utilize this best practice, you will clearly separate yourself from all other sales professionals, regardless of industry.*

Become a Trusted Advisor

If your clients view you as a trusted advisor, you will receive an abundance of referral business. The way to achieving this elite status is by solving real business problems and helping them improve their business operations with your solution. If you can operate like a free consulting resource to your client and become an extension of their staff, they will shower you with referrals.

> » **Special Blue Print Example** — *One of my largest customers viewed me as an expert in technology. They consistently sought my advice and guidance related to all aspects of technology that expanded outside of my core product set, which is telecommunications. Also, I had a badge to gain access to their building and even had my own cubicle in their IT department. This client sent me numerous referrals because they viewed me as one of their trusted advisors.*

Build Meaningful Relationships with Your Customers

The golden rule in sales is that ***people buy from people they LIKE***!

In order to build strong relationships with your customers, it is extremely important to get to know them outside of the office. Take them to lunch, dinner, and entertain them at sporting events/concerts if they are able to accept your invitation (*Many clients that work in the government sector cannot accept gifts. It is fine to extend an invitation but make sure they can legally accept your gift*). Once you are outside of the office environment, you will learn about their families, hobbies, personal interests, etc. If you can connect with your clients on a personal level, it will strengthen your overall relationship. If you have a personal relationship with your client, it will be much easier to secure referral business.

Reward Your Clients that Send You Referrals

The best way to reward clients that send referrals is to return the favor. Look for business synergies within your existing customer base to help your clients. Once you identify which of your customers need the products offered by your other customers, proactively make warm introductions. Sending referral business to your existing customers will definitely lead to more referrals!

ASK Your Clients for Referrals

This is perhaps the easiest and most overlooked aspect of securing referrals from your existing clients. If you are taking care of your customers, they will be happy to send you referral business; however, you have to **ASK**! The easiest way to accomplish this task is to sit down and make a list of all existing customers in your base that are happy with your service. Once you create this list, schedule lunch meetings, face-to-face appointments, or make phone calls, and simply ask them for referrals! You will be pleasantly surprised with the outcome. You can also design a special incentive that gives your customer a discount off their existing services if they send you referrals that lead to new clients (*obviously, this must be customize based on your company's guidelines*).

In summary, referral business is the easiest way to generate new sales. If you execute the six **Blue Print** steps above, you will create another pipeline to land new business the "**easy**" way. If you are taking care of your customers, they will take care of you! Remember, you just need to **ASK**!

Chapter 10
The Power of the Administrative Assistant
They hold the keys to the castle

**"I speak to everyone in the same way,
whether he is the garbage man or the president of the university."**

- Albert Einstein, Father Modern Physics -

Many sales professionals fail to respect the power and influence held by the administrative assistant (AA), which could be a fatal flaw in growing a strong relationship with your client. Behind the scenes, the AA directly supporting your decision-maker holds major clout within the organization. They are not directly involved in the decision-making process, but they can make a big difference in whether you win or lose a sale. Also, they are a critical factor early in the sales process because they can **block** you or **help** you land that coveted first appointment.

There are several reasons why the AA is critical to your success. They usually have supported the decision-maker for many years. As the decision-maker was promoted, started their own company, or climbed the corporate ranks, the AA moved with them and supported them throughout these many transitions. Since they have probably been working together for years, the AA is also considered a trusted advisor. Many times, the decision-maker will ask for their advice or opinion on numerous matters (*if the AA does not have a high opinion of you or receives a bad vibe, it could be detrimental to your success*).

Another significant factor is that the AA has full **CONTROL** over the decision-maker's calendar and in most cases has veto power over who they meet! Their core responsibility is to effectively manage their time and ensure they are meeting with people that can benefit the company. If they do not feel you will offer any value, they will not help you secure an appointment.

Finally, the AA is usually connected to the decision-maker's personal life outside of the office. Many times, their administrative duties bleed into the boss' activities outside of the office and they end up building a personal connection with their family, spouse, friends, etc. If they have supported your client for years, it is highly likely they are considered an extension of their family, which is why this person must be on your side.

Now that you clearly understand the importance of the AA, I will expand on ways to win their favor. If you can gain the backing of this pivotal person, it will indirectly help your sales efforts.

I would like to present four tips to score major points with the AA. **First and foremost**, always treat the AA with the utmost respect. Make sure you give them the same level of respect as the decision-maker. **Second**, always send a "written thank you card" and follow up email at the conclusion of your first meeting with the decision-maker. A short note thanking them for scheduling your meeting will ensure they remember and help you gain future access. **Third**, always take a gift for the AA during your first interaction. This gift should be small but impactful. A good example would be a beautiful plant or flowers they can display on their desk, a nice coffee mug with your company logo, or chocolate candy (*administrative assistants usually always like chocolate*). **Finally**, always give them one of your business cards. This gesture is extremely professional, classy, and demonstrates that you respect them.

> » **Special Blue Print Tip** — *In your follow up email and "written thank you card" to the AA, make sure you indicate the positive outcome of your meeting with the decision-maker and how you can help their company. The AA is responsible for protecting the decision-maker's calendar to guarantee he/she meets with people that add value. If you communicate how you can help, it will make it much easier to gain future access to the decision-maker's calendar and accelerate the sales process. Also, make sure you include your business card within your written thank you card.*

Now that I'm an executive within a Fortune 100 company, I am fortunate to have my very own Administrative Assistant. She is a wonderful lady that holds considerable influence across my sphere of responsibility. She has total control over my calendar. Many times, appointments will pop up on my calendar that I did not schedule. When I ask her about the meeting, she will simply tell me "*Reggie — this meeting is definitely worth your time.*" Because I trust her judgment, I take the meeting. This is the same process that takes place with the business owners and C-Level executives you are targeting. The point I am making is that once you establish trust and demonstrate value to the AA, you can contact them directly to schedule meetings with the decision-maker without their involvement. There are several folks within my world that work directly with my AA to schedule time on my calendar because she knows they will add value to my job.

In conclusion, the AA holds the keys to the castle and can make or break your success selling your product or service to their company. If you treat them like gold, make a good impression, and win their favor, it will dramatically help your sales efforts.

Chapter 11
The Importance of Reading on a Regular Basis

"No matter how busy you may think you are,
you must find time for reading,
or surrender yourself to self-chosen ignorance."

- Confucius, Chinese Philosopher -

Life moves fast and we are all super busy. As a sales professional, you are overwhelmed with email traffic, voice mails, text messages, demands from high maintenance clients, administrative tasks, and the burden of a monthly quota hanging over your head. A majority of your emails require action from your clients and management chain. Add in your personal life and family obligations, twenty four hours is just not enough time in the day. Despite these challenges, an essential part of your success is making time to **READ** on a daily basis.

Without reading, your capacity to discuss a wide variety of topics is drastically limited. Also, your ability to demonstrate the "**IT**" factor (*the unique skill to capture someone's attention and maintain their interest*) and generate interest and intrigue with your clients will be lost.

When I think of a well read sales professional with the ability to hold discussions across a wide variety of interesting topics, I think about "**The Most Interesting Man in the World**." I love the marketing campaign by Dos Equis beer featuring commercials starring the actor Jonathan Goldsmith as the "**The Most Interesting Man in the World**." This distinguished and well traveled gentleman is rich in stories and experiences. He is able to captivate and intrigue anyone in the world regardless of stature or title. He charms beautiful women, holds court with world dignitaries, and easily mingles within all types of unique cultures around the world. You can place him in any city around the globe and he will end up being the toast of the town. The entire premise of these charming commercials is that "**The Most Interesting Man in the World**" and Dos Equis beer both share the perspective that life should be interesting and lived to fullest. This marketing campaign is so compelling that it helped boost Dos Equis beer's domestic sales in the US by 22% since 2006 when sales of other imported beers fell by 4%. I can guarantee you that **"The Most Interesting Man in the World"** reads on a consistent basis!

It pains me to hear sales professionals ask the same old lame questions when they are attempting to break the ice with their clients. Here are a few examples of these tired questions — *how is the weather today, how is your day going, did you catch the game last night, and how about the Dallas Cowboys?*

I can understand asking these questions when the time is appropriate; however, many of these depthless questions are used to generate conversation because the sales professional has little or no interesting conversational material to reference. The ability to connect with your client is based on the information in your mental library. Reading on a consistent basis fills the subject matter in your cerebral repository with stimulating material. It also clearly separates an average sales rep from a winning professional that can demonstrate the **IT FACTOR** on a consistent basis through interesting and thought provoking conversation!

If you read on a consistent basis, imagine the depth of your conversation if you followed your client's stock performance, recent press releases, trends of their competitors, and developments in the financial markets that impact their business. Envision how strong your interaction would be if you visited your client's facebook or LinkedIn page and knew their personal interests and then searched for interesting articles or stories that provide relevant goodies to discuss about their passions or hobbies. Finally, think about the compelling nature of your interaction if you researched their favorite sports team and intelligently referenced data about their team (*people are super passionate about their favorite sports team or athlete*). These tidbits will capture their interest, lead to profound conversations, and help you connect on a deeper level.

Always remember that you are an Account "**Executive**." You are the CEO of your own company and it is imperative to read in order to be perceived as a peer to the senior level decision-makers and business owners you are calling on. If you can discuss a variety of topics that cover business, politics, social issues, and sports, it will go a long way to engage in meaningful conversations that will assist in establishing credibility and solidifying relationships with your clients.

> » **Special Blue Print Tip** — *I strongly recommend that you NEVER discuss politics and religion with your clients. These volatile subjects can quickly ruin your relationship, especially if you do not agree with their point of view. Politics and religion are extremely sensitive and personal matters that have started wars and ended friendships! STEER CLEAR OF THESE TWO TOPICS!*

Here are several resources I recommend you leverage to broaden your horizons — the **Wall Street Journal**, **USA Today**, your **local news paper** (since I reside in Dallas, I stay current on the Dallas Morning News), your **local business journal** (I read the Dallas Business Journal and Fort Worth Business Press), the **New York Times, CNN.com, CNBC.com, Fortune. com**, and any **web site that is relevant to your respective industry** (for example, I visit **fiercewireless.com**, which is a comprehensive web site focused on the wireless technology industry).

Monthly or weekly magazine subscriptions are another way to stay current. I strongly recommend that you subscribe to one or two of the following magazines — **Time, Fortune**, & **Business Week**.

Another powerful tool is **iGoogle**. iGoogle is a personalized home page that allows you to customize and display all of the web sites that you view on a regular basis in one place. It will list all of your essential news sources and captures the top five stories on each web site. This is a helpful tool that will allow you to spend less than 30 minutes of your day staying current on numerous topics by visiting a single place.

I currently have the following web sites featured on my customized iGoogle page — *CNN.com, CNBC.com, Wall Street Journal.com, New York Times.com, Forbes.com, Dallas Business Journal.com, Fiercewireless.com, ESPN.com, Weather.com, US financial stock market performance (I track the performance of all major US markets — Dow Jones Industrial, NASDAQ, and S&P 500), and my personal stock portfolio (I track the stock performance of my company, my competitors, my important clients that are publicly traded, and all companies that I personally invest in).* Each time I connect to the internet, iGoogle pops up as my home page. I spend the first part of my day glancing at this site and reading any articles that may enhance my knowledge or impact how I run my business. This process takes less than 30 minutes of my time and keeps me informed!

> » **Special Blue Print Tip** — *I strongly recommend that you add a powerful tool called Google Alerts to your arsenal. This tool will monitor the internet for new information about your existing and prospective clients (press releases, news articles, etc.) and send a proactive email alert based on how often you request the data. It is extremely easy to set up. You merely enter the names of the companies or people you want to follow and Google Alerts will automatically email you all pertinent information related to them. Google Alerts allows you to set the frequency of the alert to arrive once per day, once per week, and even as news happens. You can also use Google Alerts to stay current on your competition or respective industry. To learn more about this phenomenal tool, please visit www.google.com/alerts.*

I would now like to cover four best practices to ensure you READ each and every day. **First**, do **<u>NOT</u>** start your day without reading. You must begin your day by reading for a minimum of 30 minutes. Within this short time frame, you can cover a variety of diverse stories to enrich and diversify your knowledge of many subjects.

Second, force yourself to read a minimum of three articles per day, which takes less than 30 minutes of your time. I recommend that you read one article related to your industry, another article related to an essential trend in the business world that impacts all industries, and finally an article of your choice. I usually pick something from the sporting world since I LOVE sports!

Third, create an iGoogle page with all of your primary news sources and make this the default home page on your Internet browser. This action will force you to glance at the top five headlines across many relevant websites on a daily basis. Even if you cannot read each article, this process will provide cursory knowledge of current events in a variety of different areas. We covered this subject earlier in this chapter.

Last but definitely not least, watch the news everyday (*local or national*)! This best practice will enhance and provide more details to the articles you skim or do not have time to read in detail during your 30 minute daily reading session. I will expand on this subject shortly.

One final topic we need to visit related to reading is television. In today's information age, what you watch on TV is just as important as what you read. TV is an excellent way to supplement your daily reading. This source of data can complement and enhance many of the articles and subjects required to improve your business acumen and increase the depth of your conversations.

> » **Special <u>Blue Print</u> Tip** — *If your main source of TV viewing comes from sports, entertainment, and reality TV shows, I strongly encourage you to change. These shows are fantastic outlets to satisfy your thirst for entertainment; however, they do little to enhance the depth of your conversations with high powered executives and business owners.*

Here are some excellent channels and TV programs to watch on a consistent basis — CNBC (*from 6 AM to 12 PM, this is one of the BEST channels to watch. Their programming is 100% targeted to keep you updated on impactful business news, trends in the world economy, and the real-time performance of the financial markets*), CNN, 60 Minutes, Bloomberg, and the Local News.

"Today a reader, tomorrow a leader."

- Margaret Fuller, Writer, Journalist, and Philosopher—

Once you make reading part of your daily routine, the depth and substance of your conversations will increase. Imagine the interest you can generate with the ability to lead intelligent discussions on a wide variety of business trends impacting the US economy, social issues changing our society, sporting trends that impact your client's favorite team, and interesting stories/articles about your client's favorite causes.

» **Special <u>Blue Print</u> Example** — *Prior to a big appointment with the CEO of one of my largest accounts, I reviewed his personal pages on LinkedIn and Facebook. I learned that he was passionate about fly fishing. I researched numerous facts on fly fishing and popular places to visit for this activity. We spent the first 15 minutes of our meeting chatting about fly fishing and the remainder of the meeting was very laid back. It was an awesome ice-breaker and the CEO felt very at ease with me because we shared a meaningful conversation about fly fishing, something he loved to do. I ended up winning this client's business and building a strong relationship with the chief shot-caller based on my preparation.*

In summary, reading will improve your business acumen, increase the depth of your conversations, and help you stay current on your client's business operations. Just like "**The Most Interesting Man in the World**," reading will make you a more alluring person and help you establish deeper connections with your clients. Remember that people buy from people. If people find you interesting and captivating, they will enjoy your company which will improve the probability they will buy from you. The key to unlocking your intrigue is to **READ** on a consistent basis!

PART 3
Executing the **Blue Print**

Chapter 12
Developing & Executing a Contact Plan
*The Essence of the **Blue Print***

"A good system shortens the road to the goal."

- Orison Swett Marden, Writer and American Author -

The contact plan is one of the most significant pillars of the **Blue Print** and reminds me of playing football in college. Prior to my freshman year, Morehouse College had not assembled a winning football season in decades. Morehouse is an elite liberal arts institution focused on academics and building future African-American leaders. It has produced a long list of prominent African-American educators, corporate executives, entrepreneurs, doctors, politicians, and lawyers. It is also one of the best feeder schools for elite Ivy League graduate schools among Historically Black Colleges and Universities. Martin Luther King Jr., Spike Lee, Samuel Jackson, David Satcher, Maynard Jackson, and Cedric Richmond are a few of our distinguished alumni (*hopefully, one day they will list my name among the our distinguished alumni*). Unfortunately, the success of the football program was given little attention and we became the doormat that our rivals gladly scheduled for homecoming to guarantee an easy victory.

During the summer before the start of my freshman season, Morehouse decided to make the success of our football program a priority and end our reign as the sacrificial lamb for other Historically Black Colleges and Universities. The President of our college hired an aggressive coach and gave him the ability to recruit and offer athletic scholarships. I was one of his first blue chip recruits.

When I hit campus for summer practice, I distinctly remember being shocked by the pessimistic attitude of everyone in the football program, especially the upperclassman who were used to losing. Coach Craig Cason was faced with the daunting challenge of revitalizing the culture and attitude of the entire football program. His main ingredient to rebuilding our program and elevating expectations was executing a game plan built on organization, hard work, consistency, and positive energy. The new motto for our football program was "**THE PRIDE IS**

BACK." This phrase was prominently displayed at the entrance of our football complex directly underneath the face of a roaring Maroon Tiger (*our school mascot*). Every member of the football program was required to slap the motto when we entered and departed the facility as a clear reminder of our new attitude! The team bought into this concept and Morehouse produced the first winning football season in decades during my freshman year. Since then, Morehouse has produced a long string of triumphant seasons and recently had one of our alumni (Ramon Harewood) drafted by the Baltimore Ravens in the 2010 National Football League draft!

I used this same concept and philosophy to create the **Contact Plan**. This **Blue Print** concept is critical to penetrating a new market, growing an existing account base, and targeting new logo accounts. Here is my definition of a contact plan:

*A strategic method to establish presence and familiarity with a potential client. This focused approach requires organization, consistency, and persistence. Finally, you must be **fearless, relentless, and aggressive!***

In order to carry out an effective contact plan, you must embrace the following concept:

No One Is Going To Call You Back! You must create the opportunity!

Going forward, you must eliminate the word **"NO"** from your vocabulary and train yourself to believe that the word **"NO"** actually means **"YES."** When you are prospecting for new business, it may actually take up to eight NOs before you land an appointment with a new prospect and hear the magical word **"YES."** Also, you cannot take rejection personal or allow this negative sensation to break your internal spirit. As a sales professional, rejection means that you did not properly explain how your product can provide a unique benefit. This is why you must eliminate rejection from your mind, stay determined, and aggressively work your contact plan!

The fundamental aspect of an excellent contact plan is to develop an organized approach to penetrate a new client. This requires the use of multiple contact methods to reach a prospect (*emails, phone calls, drive-bys, written letters sent via FedEx, etc.*). You must also be extremely persistent with your follow up by consistently "touching" the same contacts within the company multiple ways on a frequent but respectful basis. Finally, you will need to build a tracking system to document each time you touch a prospect. This systematic process will let you know "who" you called, "when" you called, and "what" you said.

The next critical aspect of a solid contact plan is formulating a strategy to attack your sales territory, account deck, customer base, etc. I will now cover **seven** essential concepts to accomplish strategy.

First and foremost, you must create a defined prospect list. This is an inventory of the companies that are a perfect fit for your product or service. You must intimately know every prospect on this list and make a consistent effort to penetrate these accounts.

Second, identify the decision-makers and main influencers that impact the buying process at all of the companies on your prospect list. This will take some research on your part but hopefully you already know the titles and positions of the individuals that usually have purchasing authority for what you sell. For example, the Chief Information Officer (CIO) and Chief Financial Officer (CFO) usually make the buying decisions in the technology space.

Third, diversify the portfolio of prospects on your target list. You need to pursue large, medium, and small prospects. The larger prospects have a much longer sales cycle while the smaller prospects close much faster. Just like managing your financial portfolio, you must spread your time investment across different company sizes so all of your eggs are not in one basket.

Fourth, focus on more than just the traditional department that buys your service. In the technology industry, this would be the IT department. You must discover the decision maker that owns the responsibility for employees that need your product/service. For example, let's say I am attempting to sell a wireless data solution to a company with a nationwide sales force. The person that owns the workforce that needs my product is the VP of Sales. This would be a good person to call on in addition to the IT department especially since the IT department supports the outside sales force.

Fifth, research your prospects before calling them by reviewing their corporate website, learning about the person you are targeting (*google them, visit their Facebook/LinkedIn site, and see if they have a Twitter account*). This will allow you to build a strong connection once you reach them and enhance the conversation.

Sixth, target the competitors in the same industry as your existing customers. You should know their business well and be able to confidently speak about how your company can help.

Last but definitely not least, focus on industry verticals or specific industries where your company has excelled. I am referring to industries proven to rely on your product/solution such as transportation, healthcare, government, construction, manufacturing, etc. A perfect example would be if you are selling an on-line dating service, a perfect target would be single ladies, single guys, and divorcees looking to rebound. Another example is a sales professional that sells custom swimming pools. A perfect target would be high-end subdivisions in Dallas, TX where people may have disposal income and the weather is scorching hot! Obviously, you will need to customize this approach to fit your industry but hopefully you understand the concept.

> **Special Blue Print Tip** — *In the technology business, many sales professionals get stuck in the IT department because this group traditionally makes the buying decisions. The most successful reps in my profession expand outside of IT and target the actual business unit that will be using our product. For example, if we are selling a mobile solution that gives field service technicians the ability to access corporate data remotely, it is important to target the CIO **AND** the VP of Field Services (the actual field service technician will have a BIG impact/influence over the final decision). I strongly encourage you to get outside your comfort zone and focus on the senior executive whose organization will be using your product or service in addition to calling on the traditional decision-maker that usually buys your solution.*

I will now present the essence of the **BLUE PRINT**! Here are the six proven steps to penetrate a new prospect:

Prospecting 101

- The Six Steps to Success -

The Blue Print

Step #1 — The Infamous Cold Call — LEAVE A VOICE MAIL

Step #2 — Immediate Follow Up Email — Keep It Short

Step #3 — 2nd Cold Call — Leave another Voice Mail

Step #4 — 2nd Follow Up Email — Be Concise

Step #5 — Unannounced Appointment — The Infamous "Drive-By"

Step #6 — Immediate Follow Up Email — Keep It Short

...If you don't land an appointment after Step #6, start the process all over again...

In order to properly execute the six steps of the **Blue Print**, you must leave a voice mail after **ALL** phone calls. This is an opportunity for the client to hear your voice as you clearly describe who you are and why you are calling. Even if they delete your voice mail, it will trigger their memory and establish familiarity when you send a follow up email. Next, you must send all follow-up emails within **24 to 48** hours after your call or drive-by. If you do not send an email follow up, you have wasted an opportunity to make a quality touch. Finally, you must consistently touch the prospect every two to three weeks so they will not forget about you.

In conclusion, formulating a solid contact plan is a critical step to properly executing the **Blue Print**. This process will help you connect with a potential client, further penetrate your respective market, grow an existing account base, and successfully target new logo accounts. Remember, it may take numerous touches to land your first appointment. This process allows you to build familiarity as you work to secure that precious meeting. These potential clients will routinely hear your pleasant voice mails, receive your concise emails, and be impressed by your clever gifts. Eventually, chance will be on your side and you will catch them at the right time. When you do, they will feel like they already have a relationship with you and accept your meeting invitation! If you complete this focused approach in a consistent manner, the spoils of victory will be yours!

Chapter 13
The Infamous "Drive-By"
The BEST Way to Secure an Appointment

"The fishermen know that the sea is dangerous and the storm terrible, but they have never found those dangers reason for remaining ashore."

- Vincent van Gogh, Dutch Painter -

DRIVE-BYs are the BEST way to land a customer facing appointment. People can hide behind the phone, escape behind voice mail, easily delete your emails, discard your written letters — **BUT** — you seriously diminish their ability to hide when you show up in person at their office with a big SMILE.

If you are sharply dressed, smile, display positive energy, and treat the receptionist (*or other gatekeeper*) with respect, you have a super opportunity to actually speak to the decision-maker in person during your visit and book a formal appointment. Another benefit is the chance to discover essential facts to expedite the sales cycle. Finally, it is highly likely the decision-maker will actually visit with you because they already know you through your many contact points (*voice mails, emails, etc.*), that is, if you consistently executed the contact plan we reviewed in the previous chapter.

You must be **FEARLESS** in your approach and possess major courage in order to conduct drive-bys! Here is the definition of a drive-by:

An unannounced, in-person visit to the customer's office where the sales professional takes a creative gift, attempts to land an appointment, befriends the decision-maker's personal assistant, and gathers information critical to expediting the sales process. The sales professional is confident, exudes positive energy, and goes with the **INTENT** *to secure the appointment!*

When I started my career in professional sales, I watched the original version of the movie "Wall Street," which is a movie released in 1987 by 20th Century Fox. It was directed by Oliver Stone and stars Michael Douglas, Charlie Sheen, and Daryl Hannah. I was inspired by the tenacity and relentless focus of the main character "Bud Fox," played by Charlie Sheen. From this movie, I devised my concept of the drive-by.

Here is a synopsis of the scene in the movie that inspired me to create the DRIVE-BY:

Bud Fox (Charlie Sheen), a junior stockbroker is desperate to become a millionaire and Wall Street legend. Gordon Gekko (played by Michael Douglas), is a ruthless and legendary Wall Street player and one of the wealthiest men in NYC. Bud Fox called Gordon Gekko 52 days straight but did not receive a return call. Each time he called, he purposely befriended Gekko's personal assistant, Natalie. Realizing that his phone calls were a dead end, he decided to conduct a drive-by on Gekko's birthday. Prior to conducting this drive-by, he read an article in Fortune Magazine featuring Gekko and knew he loved exotic Cuban cigars. Bud Fox went to Gekko's office with Cuban cigars as his attention-grabbing gift and pushed for an appointment. Because he was always friendly and respectful to Natalie and asked to "personally" hand deliver his special cigars, she agreed to give him 5 minutes with Gekko! This chance meeting allowed Bud Fox to land Gekko as his client.

This scene inspired me to add drive-bys to my contact plan. If Bud Fox did not have the courage to carry out the drive by, he would have NEVER landed this meeting with Gordon Gekko.

We will now review the fundamentals to execute this strategy. First and foremost, you must look professional and well-groomed. A wise man once said that if you look good, people will always treat you nice and show you respect. Gentleman need to wear a shirt and tie and ladies need to wear a business suit (*Guys — if you are not willing to wear a suit and tie, please wear a sports jacket*). Next, you must walk and talk with confidence. People are captivated by confidence. Finally, always smile. A glowing smile permeates positive energy and people will respond much more favorable if you flash your pearly whites.

Always take a CREATIVE gift and a customized information packet (*specific data detailing how your company can help this client*) during your visit. Your clever gift does not have to be expensive rather something memorable that will grab their attention and help them recall your name when you follow up via email and phone call. We will cover the art of developing clever gifts later in this chapter.

Once you look nice and have an outstanding gift/customized information packet in hand, attack this activity with the INTENT to secure the appointment! When you conduct your drive-bys, your goal is to touch the decision-maker and schedule a meeting. Make sure you approach each and every drive-by with this objective!

Another critical aspect of the drive-by is befriending the receptionist and treating this person like **GOLD.** Do not under-estimate the power of the receptionist. In many companies, this individual is the glue in the office and wears many hats. They have visibility into the entire organization and know the comings and goings of everyone in the company. They are a highly respected individual because they are responsible for setting the tone for how people view the company during their visit to the corporate office. One of the biggest accounts I closed (*large fortune 1,000 company which resulted in $2.5 million of new revenue for Sprint*) was due to my relationship with the receptionist. Each time I called or did a drive-by to their corporate office, I always treated her with respect. She helped me secure my first appointment with the company's entire IT staff and also ensured that the CIO attended the first meeting. If you are friendly and respectful to the receptionist, they will aid your sales efforts. Finally, memorize the receptionist's name. If you have to call back or conduct another drive-by, they will be more inclined to help you because you addressed them by first name!

If the person you are trying reach is unavailable, always ask to speak directly with their Administrative Assistant. If you do have the opportunity to speak directly with their AA, make sure you sell yourself directly to this person. Tell them how you can help their company and why a meeting with the decision-maker is a valuable use of their time. As we discussed in a previous chapter entitled "*The Power of the Administrative Assistant*," this power broker controls the decision-maker's calendar. If they believe you can offer their company value and help their boss, they will help you land that precious meeting.

Do not become discouraged if the decision-maker is not available. Remember — *you are targeting very busy people with vast levels of responsibility*. It is not uncommon that they will be in a meeting, out of the office, or on a conference call. If this happens, there are several ways to maximize your time and turn this trip into a positive experience that helps you move closer to securing that prized appointment. I will now cover three brilliant tips for an effective drive-by.

First, leave a hand-written note for the decision-maker. Personally write a short note directly to the person you are there to see and leave it with your drive-by gift. Also, stress the importance of making sure your gift/information packet reaches the decision-maker by making the following statement to the receptionist — "*Can you please make sure Mrs. X receives this extremely important package? It is very critical that they receive my gift, personal note, and information packet. Can I count on you to ensure it reaches her desk?*" This personal touch will ensure that your gift/information packet actually reaches the decision-maker.

Second, while you are at the customer's office, do not be afraid to ask questions and secure more details about the point of contact you are trying to reach. These questions will help you uncover the following critical data — *are you calling on the right person, what is the best time to call, what are some better ways to reach them, who else is involved in the decision-making process?* You can also ask the receptionist for tips to land an appointment. Here are a few ways to approach this delicate task — *"I have been working very hard to secure a meeting with Ms. CEO. Do you have any suggestions or tips that will help me secure an appointment? I know I can be a valuable asset to your company. Can you please help me?"* If you look good, smile, and treat the receptionist like gold, it will be very hard for that person to say no and not be willing to help you. Any tip from this influential person will aid your efforts to land that treasured meeting.

Finally, communicate the importance of your visit. When you introduce yourself to the receptionist or point of contact, here is a compelling statement to make — *"You are one of the most important prospects in my sales territory and it is critical for me to build a partnership with your company. I am confident I can be a valuable resource to your company and help you gain a competitive advantage in the XXX industry. All I am asking for is an opportunity to prove myself. I'm certain that Mr. CEO will find our meeting extremely useful."* Also, leave your business card with everyone you meet. The more people that you encounter will increase the chance that your point of contact will know that you were making another respectful attempt to reach them. Imagine the buzz around the water cooler you will create if you are sharply dressed, respectful, and come with a creative gift. Also, if you exude positive energy topped off with a bright smile, the decision maker will mostly likely know you were there if you meet as many people as you can during your visit.

> » **Special Blue Print Tip** — *Give a small gift to the receptionist of your most important customers and prospects. During my tenure as a Sales Manager, one of my successful sales reps conducted over five drive-bys before landing a first appointment with one of his key clients. He had visited the office so many times that the receptionist had five different coffee mugs on her desk with our company logo. The cool thing about this story is that she prominently displayed these coffee mugs so everyone that entered and exited the office could see them. She was very instrumental in helping this sales professional land his first appointment with the decision-maker, which led to eventually winning all of their business!*

The next concept related to the drive-by is making this activity a routine part of your business. The most successful sales professionals I know conduct drive-bys after ALL customer facing appointments. This best practice will also make you more productive. In many cases, you are traveling several miles to visit your existing customers. It makes perfect sense to maximize your time and hit all prospects in that given area since you are already there.

The execution of this "money-making" strategy does require organization, planning, and research. Prior to your appointment, you will need to analyze the geographic area where your existing customer is located and determine what other companies in this same ten mile radius are solid prospects for your product/service. You can use Hoovers, Business Wise (*if located in Atlanta, DFW, or Charlotte*), or another business tool to scrub the area (*Hoovers & Business Wise both have a search function that will allow you to find "like" companies in the same zip code, building, office park, or street*). Next, you must dedicate time to prepare your drive-by gifts and customized information packets to deliver while you are in the area. After completing these easy steps, you will be prepared to conduct drive-bys before or after your appointments to maximize your time. Finally, you will be able to include other resources on your drive-bys to help you land that first appointment since these folks will already be out in the field with you. Teaming with your sales manager or another co-worker that attended your meeting is fun and educational as you can debrief immediately after the drive-by to see what worked and what didn't work.

> » **Special Blue Print Tip** — *If you want to make BIG money, I challenge you to conduct a minimum of **ONE** drive-by after every customer facing appointment! If you are willing to add this best practice to your standard routine, you will become more productive, always have a robust sales funnel, and make BIG deposits into your bank account.*

Weak Gifts + Low Creativity = NO Response...

The next concept crucial to the drive-by is delivering a **CREATIVE GIFT**. Most sales professionals only take information packets which are usually always discarded, not read, piled up in the decision-makers mailbox, or thrown in the trash can. If you take a clever gift, you increase the chance that your information packet and hand-written note will reach the decision-maker.

Over the past eight years, I've had the pleasure to witness several unique gifts in action. Some of these gifts may be corny but the intent is to catch someone's attention and help you stand out! Also, I strongly encourage you to leave a picture of yourself on some of the gifts when appropriate (*another way to establish a connection and familiarity*).

Here is a list of awesome gifts that work — *doughnuts (everyone **LOVES** these tasty treats in the morning), cupcakes (you can have a local bakery customize your cupcakes with your company logo), large cookie with your personal contact information written on the cookie in frosting (most baker- ies can customize this leave-behind for you), coffee mug with your company's logo stuffed with candy (receptionists love Hershey's Kisses), $10 Starbucks gift card, bagels, message in a bottle (with a personalized message and your contact information), chocolate chess set (with a message entitled "it's your move"), fruit basket, really nice plant, beautiful flower arrangement, flower pot with soil and seeds (with a message entitled "Let's grow our business relationship together"), box of chocolates, a special "To-Do" list with a note pad inscribed with your company's logo and a really nice pin (#1 item on the to-do list is to call you and schedule an appointment), an actual puzzle with a message around how you can solve problems, and a small piggy bank with a message centered around saving money/reducing costs.*

> » **Special Blue Print Tip** — *Remember to have fun! If you let your imagination flow, I am confident you will develop some really cool goodies to leave with your prospects! Find out what they like through research (Facebook, LinkedIn, Twitter, their executive assistant, the receptionist, etc.) and personalize your gift. If you are willing to unleash your creative side, you will vastly increase your chance to catch the decision-maker's attention.*

During the special seasons throughout the year, I encourage you to leverage these different and unique seasonal themes. Here are the most popular holidays to focus on — *Christmas, Thanksgiving, Halloween, NFL Super Bowl, March Madness/NCAA basketball championship tournament, Valentine's Day, Easter, Mardi Gras, the beginning of Spring, Spring Break, Summertime, the beginning of Fall, Memorial Day, 4th of July, Labor Day, & the New Year.*

> » **Special Blue Print Tip** — *I have a Christmas season special for you to execute. During the holiday season, don a Santa Claus cap during your drive-bys and wrap your info packet like a present (Santa is here to deliver gifts). This will really catch everyone's attention in the office and give you direct access to the decision- maker if he or she is in the office that day.*

It is now time to **SHOW YOU THE MONEY**! To effectively demon- strate the power of this essential activity, I would like to quantify how much money each Drive-By is worth to you. We covered this concept in a previous chapter entitled — "*The Importance of Time Management.*" However, it is extremely powerful to relate time and money to conduct- ing routine drive-bys.

Here are some assumptions to use to calculate the value of each Drive-By:

- Based on making **$200,000** per year in total compensation

- Based on a monthly goal of **32** Customer-Facing Appointments to attend each month

- Primary Assumption — **it takes 5 Drive-Bys to secure 1 appointment**

Here is the magic formula:

- How much is each New Appointment worth? — **$521** (*Formula — 32 appointments x 12 months = 384 Total Appointments per year — $200,000/384 = $521*)

- How much is each Drive-By worth? — **$104.20** (*Formula — $521 — divided by- 5 Drive-bys = $104.20*)

Based on this math and a goal of making **$200,000**, each Drive-By is worth **$104.20**. So, look in the mirror before you start your day and ask yourself the following questions — *Do I want to get paid, do I want to dominate the market, am I ready to make **$1,563** today (15 Drive-Bys x $104.20)?*

To conclude this vital discussion, I want to leave you with an email chain that clearly validates the power of the DRIVE-BY. This sales rep referenced in this email did a routine drive-by with a simple batch of cookies that resulted in Sprint winning a significant wireless contract for one of the largest advertising companies in the US. This multi-million dollar account resulted in this sales rep achieving President's Council and earning a life changing commission check!

Follow up Email 24 Hours after the Drive-By

Jeff,

I am sorry I missed you when I stopped by your office. I hope you enjoyed the tasty Savannah cookies! I am a Sprint Account Executive in your area. My ultimate goal is to understand your business and help you leverage technology to be more productive. I would like to schedule a meeting to learn more about your strategic direction and determine how Sprint can be a resource to you. Please advise which date best fits your calendar:

- ***Tuesday March 6th @ 2 PM***

- ***Wednesday March 7th @ 10AM or 2 PM***

- *Friday March 9th @ 10AM or 2 PM*

Also, my Solutions Engineer will be joining us to provide a technology update on wireless broadband technology. I strongly believe that this will be a valuable use of your time. Thank you in advance and I look forward to meeting with you.

Best Regards,

Betsy

Customer Response

Betsy,

First, thanks so much for your note and for the cookies — we are longtime Byrd Cookie Company fans! If we could meet on Tuesday, March 6th at 2:00, that would work best for us. We will be joined by my Director of Network Operations, my Senior Manager of Desktop Support, and our IT Procurement Coordinator.

Just so you are aware, our primary spend in the wireless space is with one of your main competitors. While we are open to considering other alternatives going forward, they have a pretty good sized footprint within our organization.

My executive assistant is copied on this note and will assist you if there is anything that you need to coordinate for the meeting. Thanks, and I look forward to meeting you.

Vice President, CIO

In conclusion, Drive-Bys are the most effective way to secure new appointments and make a positive impression with your clients! In order to catch the decision-maker's attention, you must take a creative gift! These "attention-grabbers" will ensure the client remembers your name and pave the way for that coveted appointment. Finally, each door you knock on is worth money in your back account! Have fun, smile, and exploit your artistic talents! If you make Drive-Bys part of your normal routine, you will vastly increase your sales results!

Chapter 14
The Art of Telemarketing
Cold Calling Tactics That Work

"Where one door is shut, another is opened."

- Miguel de Cervantes, Spanish Writer -

I will be the first to admit, cold calling is not one of my favorite activities. Performing this grueling task on a daily basis is very tough work! Unfortunately, it is a necessary evil and critical to succeeding in professional sales. If you cannot use an existing relationship from your personal/professional network or you do not have an existing client that can make a warm introduction, you must go in **COLD**.

When I started my career in professional sales, I was inspired by a particular scene from the movie, "Boiler Room," featuring Ben Affleck. He played a sales trainer for a stock brokerage firm. His job was to train all new stockbrokers joining his firm the art of telemarketing. From this movie, I built the necessary confidence to make winning cold calls and make this necessary evil a main part of my contact plan.

Here is a synopsis of the scene in the movie that was my source of inspiration. In this scene, Ben Affleck was disappointed by the production of his "new hire" class and gave them a motivational speech to fire them up:

"Get on the phones, it's time to get to work. Get off your butts!!!! Move around, motion creates emotion. I remember I had this guy call me up and try and to pitch me some stock. So I let him…I got every rebuttal out of this guy and kept him on the phone for 90 minutes. Towards the end of the call, I started asking him buying questions — Like, what's the firm's minimum? — that's a buying question. Right there, that guy's gotta take me down. I was giving him a run and he blew it. To a question like what is the firm's minimum, the answer is ZERO. You don't like the idea, don't pick up a single share. You have to be closing ALL of the TIME! Be aggressive…learn how to PUSH. Talk to him…ask him questions…ask him rhetorical questions…ask him anything, it doesn't matter, just get a YES out of him. If you are drowning and I throw you a life jacket, would you grab it? YES. Good, then pick up 200 hundred shares,

I won't let you down. Ask him if he would like to see 30% returns...what's he gonna say...No?

Have your rebuttals ready... if the guy says call me tomorrow...that's BS... someone tells you they have money problems buying 200 hundred shares is lying to you...You know how I respond to that? I say look man, tell me you don't like my firm...Tell me you don't like my idea...Tell me you don't like my freakin' neck-tie...but don't tell me you can't put together $2,500.

There is NO such thing as a NO sales call...A Sale is made on every call you make...either you sell the client some stock OR he sells you on a reason why he can't...Either way, a sale is made. The only question is who is gonna close? You or him? Now be relentless...That's it...I'm done!"

From this scene, I would constantly remind myself during each telemarketing session:

There is NO such thing as a **"NO" SALES CALL**....*either you sell the client on why they should see you, or they sell you on a reason why they can't....either way, a SALE is made! It's you or them....so be RELENTLESS!*

Many sales professionals make the task of telemarketing way too complicated. Telemarketing is very simple! Introduce yourself, get straight to the point, and ask for the meeting. Most C-level executives and business owners have spent time in sales. And like the Russian proverb, *"One fisherman sees another fisherman from afar,"* they appreciate the fact that you have the courage to be in sales and they respect how you earn your living! If you are confident, polite, and concise, they will give you a few minutes of their time before putting up their guard.

Before moving on, I would like to cover nine basic **Blue Print** fundamentals to executing the infamous **COLD CALL**. These will definitely improve your odds on landing customer appointments while conducting this grueling exercise.

First and foremost, keep it simple! Many sales professionals make telemarketing a mystifying experience. I'm a firm believer that cold calling is very straight forward. You are merely having a formal conversation with another educated person that happens to be a stranger. With that said, it is essential to be clever and have fun. I encourage you to **SMILE** while you are making cold calls. A simple smile exudes confidence, passion, and energy through the telephone (*buy a small mirror and keep it in front of you while making calls to ensure you keep a big smile on your face*). The positive energy that permeates through the phone will increase your probability to land more appointments while cold calling.

Second, be yourself! I encourage you to relax, slow down, and use that warm personality that led you to the exciting profession of sales. Since you are merely having a conversation with another human being, do not sound "scripted" like you are reading directly from the telemarketing scripts we will review later in this chapter. Most importantly, you must communicate the passion and energy that's in your heart for the company you represent and the outstanding product/service you provide. No one wants to be around a lifeless person with zero energy. People like to be jazzed up so you must convey all of your authentic energy through the phone! You are in sales for a reason so leverage your enthusiastic personality.

Third, always introduce yourself and ask the prospect how they are doing. Remember, you are having a conversation with another human being that has feelings. A simple way to accomplish this task is to simply say *"How are you doing today?"* This small gesture will set the tone for a fruitful conversation.

Fourth, be succinct and get straight to the point. After breaking the ice, quickly communicate why you are calling and how you can help their company. Always remember that the decision-makers you are calling have little patience and are very busy. Your creditability will rise if you are concise and direct. Do not ramble or go off on tangents. After you make your intentions known, ask for the appointment! If they say no, be prepared with your rebuttals to their objections and continue to respectfully ask for the appointment.

Fifth, always lead with your company's most differentiated or hottest product. I'm confident your company's marketing department invested significant advertising dollars to make your target audience aware of these unique solutions. Since they are creating awareness, capitalize on this air cover and lead with these hot products. For example, for years AT&T was the only wireless company to offer the game-changing iPhone. Sprint secured rights to begin offering this device in Oct-2011. Since this is one of our hottest devices, our sales force is clearly communicating this differentiated product to all clients in conjunction with our ability to solve business problems via our robust technology portfolio. Another example would be if you are selling DirecTV packages to potential clients, you would definitely want to lead with the fact that you are the only provider that offers the exclusive NFL package (*this cool feature gives a football fanatic access to every single game played on Sunday, which is the main reason why I am a loyal DirecTV customer*).

Sixth, if you have resources that can attend the appointment with you, mention them. At Sprint and many other Fortune 1,000 companies, we exercise the concept of team selling, where the sales rep has a group of internal resources at their disposal to attend customer calls. If you fall into this category, make your client aware of these benefits! A simple way to tout your strong support team is to say the following — *"I plan on bringing my Solutions Engineer with me. We call him the "Jedi Master of Technology." He clearly understands how technology is used to solve real business problems. He will add value to our meeting."* Also, make sure to highlight all of the dedicated resources that will support your client. I usually emphasize this point by making the following statement — *"I lead a team of dedicated resources that will be at your disposal if you conduct business with me."* This may seem minor but it will go a long way to secure appointments especially if your competition does not offer the same level of service!

Seventh, if you receive significant push back while you have the client on the phone, secure their email address and gain permission to stay in touch on a quarterly basis by sending pertinent data specifically related to improving their business operations, trends related to their industry, and crucial data about their competition. Make sure they know that you will not spam or send them frivolous material that clogs up their in-box. One thing to convey is that you interface with a wide variety of clients which gives you perspective on what's happening in their industry. This unique perspective will allow you to share best practices and ways that similar companies are using your service to gain a competitive advantage. Securing their OK to send quarterly updates could be the initial way to get your foot in the door.

Eighth, clearly declare to the client how pivotal this meeting is to you and your company. This gesture will demonstrate the enthusiasm and passion we discussed earlier in this chapter. A good way to convey this point is to say the following — *"You are a very meaningful client to my company and building a relationship with your company is extremely important to me. All I am asking is for 30 minutes of your time. I guarantee our meeting will be a good use of your time."* You are basically guaranteeing this client that meeting with you is worth their precious time. Also, be willing to make the commitment that you will quickly end the appointment if they do not see value during the meeting. A great way to convey this point is to say the following — *"If I don't demonstrate value in 15 minutes, you can kick me out. I will get up and respectfully exit your office without any hard feelings."* This bold move will demonstrate your confidence to add value to their company!

Last but definitely not least, do not try and sell your product over the phone! Remember, we are demystifying the cold calling experience by keeping things simple. Your goal while telemarketing is to entice the client enough to close the appointment.

> » **Special Blue Print Tip** — *If you actually have a conversation or get your prospect on the phone and fail to secure the appointment, mail them a written Thank You card and send them a follow up email within 24 hours outlining your conversation and highlighting how you can help their company. Be sure to make this email short and sweet. This will help you further establish familiarity and increase your chances to land an appointment the next time you call or conduct a drive-by. The use of a written Thank You card is a powerful gesture.*

We will now review some proven telemarketing scripts to implement into your cold calling operation. Here are four fantastic versions to use:

#1 — Introduction — Generic Version

Good Afternoon _____, my name is Reggie Marable calling from Sprint. How are you doing today? (**Wait for a response**). I am a Business Consultant responsible for the Dallas/FW market. It is my responsibility to help my clients exploit technology to make more money (OR — *be more productive, gain a competitive advantage, make their employees more productive*).

The purpose of my call is to schedule time on your calendar to introduce myself in person, learn more about the business challenges you face, and determine how Sprint can be a resource to your company.

How is next Thursday at 10 AM or 2 PM for a brief 30 minute appointment?

#2 — Introduction — Industry Specific Version

Good Afternoon _____, my name is Reggie Marable calling from Sprint. How are you doing today? (**Wait for a response**) I am a Business Consultant responsible for managing Sprint's customers in the **TRANSPORTATION INDUSTRY**. It is my responsibility to help my clients exploit technology to make more money (OR — *be more productive, gain a competitive advantage, make their employees more productive*).

The purpose of my call is to schedule time on your calendar to introduce myself in person, learn more about the business challenges you face, and determine how Sprint can be a resource to your company.

How does next Thursday at 10 AM or 2 PM sound for a brief 30 minute appointment?

#3 — Second Call Attempt — Generic Version

Good Afternoon _____, my name is Reggie Marable calling from Sprint. How are you doing today? (**Wait for a response**) I am a Business Consultant responsible for the Dallas/FW market. It is my responsibility to help my clients leverage technology to make more money (OR — *be more productive, gain a competitive advantage, make their employees more productive*).

A number of weeks ago I contacted you, and you asked me to call you back today to set up an appointment. The purpose of my call is to schedule time on your calendar to introduce myself in person, learn more about the business challenges you face, and determine how Sprint can be a resource to your company.

How does next Thursday at 10 AM or 2 PM sound for a brief 30 minute appointment?

#4 — Follow Up Call after a Drive-By — Generic Version

Good Afternoon _____, my name is Reggie Marable calling from Sprint. How are you doing today? (**Wait for a response**) I stopped by your office last Monday afternoon but missed you. I hope you enjoyed the tasty chocolate treat I left with your receptionist Debbie.

I am a Business Consultant responsible for the Dallas/FW market. It is my responsibility to help my clients leverage technology to make more money (OR — *be more productive, gain a competitive advantage, make their employees more productive*).

The purpose of my call is to schedule time on your calendar to introduce myself in person, learn more about the business challenges you face, and determine how Sprint can be a resource to your company.

How does next Thursday at 10 AM or 2 PM sound for a brief 30 minute appointment?

Handling Objections

"Nothing great was ever achieved without enthusiasm."

Ralph Waldo Emerson, American Poet

The art of handling objections is an essential craft to dominate this profession. If you cannot master this critical skill, it will become extremely difficult to secure new appointments, which means you will not make any money. Objections are merely a reactionary tool used by human beings to avoid further conversation, quickly exit discussions, and shut down the person asking questions. If you do not have the prowess to overcome objections, you give people the ability to quickly dismiss you. Think about all of the sales people in the mall that work the kiosks and sell products to shoppers at the mall. Many times, I will stop and observe these sales professionals give up on the very first objection without presenting a rebuttal or even asking questions to inquire why the person they approached said no. These poor folks are usually always dismissed because they have not mastered this art.

The fundamental aspect to overcoming objections is to ask questions, understand why the customer is putting up a road block, and eloquently address the issue. Here are the top eight objections you will encounter while cold calling, which are standard across all industries:

I am already in a contract

I heard your company is struggling financially or your customer service is horrible

I had a bad experience with your company and switched my service to your competition

I am not interested

We don't have the budget and we are looking at reducing costs

Call me back in a few months

Send me some information

You need to speak with someone a few levels down

You will hear these ALL of the time whether you are selling girl scout cookies, medical equipment, or computer software! They are consistent across all industries and extremely common. In order to succeed with telemarketing, you must be able to address these common objections.

There is definitely an art to handling objections. You must ask questions to understand the customer's motivation for putting up the road block and have strong rebuttals prepared to counter them. When you are dialing for dollars, being organized is crucial to your success. You need to have your rebuttals laid out in an organized fashion so you can quickly access them when you are challenged. This will ensure your flow is natural and doesn't sound scripted. Finally, after addressing the objection, you must ask for the appointment!

I will now present some excellent rebuttals to the common objections outlined above:

I AM ALREADY IN A CONTRACT — *You will hear this objection quite often. The most effective way to handle this objection is to ask questions! Here are a few good ones to ask when encountered with this classic objection — What provider are you currently using, how are you using their service, and how are things going (is your current provider taking care of you, are they meeting your needs, how is the overall relationship, etc.)?*

These questions will help you start a productive conversation and secure the necessary information to eventually earn their business. Once you secure this material, here are four solid options to work past this objection and land the appointment.

Option #1 — I realize a company of your size/stature would already have a service provider. It is my responsibility to build a relationship with your company whether you choose to do business with me or not. I am just asking for 30 minutes of your time to get my foot in the door. At the very minimum, I can provide a brief technology update on where Sprint is going and how we are helping other companies in the **XXX** industry. Can I please have 30 minutes of your time next _____ at ___?

Option #2 — I realize a company of your size/stature would already have a service provider. My objective is to ensure that you are aware of technology advances relative to your industry and alternatives available to you. At the very minimum, I can provide a brief technology update concerning Sprint's offerings and how we are helping other companies within your industry. Would you give me 30 minutes of your time next _____ at ___?

Option #3 — All I am asking for is 30 minutes of your time to better understand your business and become an additional consulting resource. In the event you need me in the future, I will be an effective asset and be ready to support you because I understand how you operate. Plus, it is always great to have a second option and know what other solutions are available in the marketplace. Can I please have 30 minutes of your time next _____ at ___?

Option #4 — I am only asking for 30 minutes of your time. It is my responsibility to build a relationship with your company whether you choose to do business with me or not. At the very minimum, I can provide a brief update on how Sprint's technology will revolutionize how your company is operating today. It is always good to have a second option and know what other solutions are available in the marketplace. Can I please have 30 minutes of your time next _____ at ___?

I'M ALREADY IN A CONTRACT & IT IS TOO MUCH HASSLE TO CHANGE

I understand your position; however I would like to ask a few questions — *Which providers do you currently utilize, how long is your contract, if we can meet your requirements and minimize the change over impact on your business, would you consider a proposal from my company?*

We have access to an acquisition budget to help alleviate those up-front costs of moving forward with my company (**Caution — only say this if you can deliver on this commitment**). Also, we have dedicated Project Management resources to completely handle your service migration process. These dedicated resources will ensure a smooth transition and require minimal impact from your staff or disrupt your daily operations. Please give me 30 minutes of your time to better explain the process, get my foot in the door, and start building a relationship with your company. How about 30 minutes next _____ at ___?

I HEARD YOUR COMPANY IS STRUGGLING FINANCIALLY — OR — YOUR CUSTOMER SERVICE IS HORRIBLE

Best Option — Be prepared with 3 — 5 points that clearly highlight the financial strength of your company and how your company is working to improve in the customer service arena. After listing these main points, ask for the appointment.

I HAD A BAD EXPERIENCE WITH YOUR COMPANY A FEW YEARS AGO AND MOVED MY BUSINESS TO YOUR COMPETITION

Best Option — I apologize for your bad experience. I am proud to represent my company and it is very important to me to reset your expectations because we have made several positive changes over the past few years (*be prepared to list all of the major changes and improvements your company has made*). I would like to ask a few questions about why you cancelled your service — *Which provider did you switch to, why did you switch providers (obtain the specific reason), how long is your contract, can I have an opportunity to repair our relationship and re-gain your trust, if my company meets your requirements and minimizes the change over impact on your business, would you consider a proposal from us in the future, and if we can provide you with a plan to contribute to your cost reduction program, while improving business operations, would you be interested in working with me on formulating the details?*

I would like an opportunity to re-earn your trust and address the issues that caused you to leave my company. Please grant me 30 minutes of your time. How is next Thursday at 10 AM?

I AM NOT INTERESTED — *make sure you customize this rebuttal to fit your industry*

Option #1 — How much do you know about my company and the many ways we are helping our clients gain more productivity from their employees to secure a competitive advantage? I am confident that my company can be a solid resource for you. Just give me 30 minutes and I guarantee this will be good use of your time. How about next Thursday at 10 AM?

Option #2 — I know you are probably not interested in hearing just about cell phones; however, Sprint is a technology company with a wealth of products and services to improve productivity, contain costs, and make your staff more efficient. We are doing some unique and innovative things with technology. Please give me 30 minutes of your time to provide a brief technology update. I promise to demonstrate value within 15 minutes of our meeting or you can kick me out. My goal is to build a relationship and not sell you anything. How about next Thursday at 10 AM?

Option #3 — It is my goal to understand the "big picture" of where your company is going. This information will allow me to better serve your company and be a resource for you. Since you are the chief architect of your company's overall strategy, please grant me 30 minutes of your time to learn more about your goals and primary challenges. Also, I would like the opportunity to provide a brief update on how our clients (*and your competitors*) are using our technology to gain a competitive advantage in your respective industry. How about next Thursday at 10 AM?

WE JUST DON'T HAVE THE BUDGET & WE ARE LOOKING TO REDUCE COSTS — *Given the state of the economy, this is an objection you will hear quite frequently*

Best Option — In today's challenging economic conditions, I hear this concern quite often from my clients. My company has a wide variety of solutions that can help you accomplish this goal and gain more productivity from your employees. I can help you do more with less! If we can provide you with a cost-effective plan to contribute to your cost reduction goal while improving business operations, would you be interested in learning more?

CALL ME BACK IN A FEW MONTHS — OR — SEND ME SOME INFORMATION

Option #1 — You are a very important client to me. I would love to add you to my distribution list; however, I am merely asking for 30 minutes of your time to get my foot in the door and start building a relationship with your company. At the very minimum, I can provide a technology update and review the rapid changes impacting your industry today. I promise to demonstrate value during our meeting. If not, you can show me the door within 15 minutes and I will quickly depart with no hard feelings as I failed to meet your expectations. How about next Thursday at 10 AM?

Option #2 — Absolutely. I will be in your area next _____, I will put together a personalized information packet specifically designed on how I can support _____ and hand-deliver it to you in person. In addition, I will have some doughnuts and fresh coffee for your staff.

Option #3 ***IF YOU DARE, TRY THIS ONE*** — Absolutely. I have a comprehensive and interactive package of information. *If you stand it on its end, it is five feet eleven inches high and weighs 210 pounds. We call it Reggie Marable.* When do you want me there?

Option #4 — No problem. In the meantime, I would like to keep you updated on the latest and greatest technology impacting your industry (*technology is changing every day*). I have created a customized newsletter to help my customers stay ahead of the curve. I will send you this valuable information on a quarterly basis. — *I promise, I will not SPAM you.* — *Ask for their email address...*

YOU NEED TO SPEAK WITH SOMEONE A FEW LEVELS DOWN

Option #1 — It is my responsibility to build a relationship and understand the overall strategic direction of your company. I lead a team of resources that will help your company exploit technology to make more money, operate more efficiently, and better serve your customers. At the very minimum, I can provide a high level technology update as it relates to your strategic direction. Meeting with your staff will be beneficial; however, it will be extremely impactful to start with you to merge our solutions with your long-term goals. All I am asking for is 30 minutes of your time. I guarantee I will demonstrate value within 15 minutes or you can kick me out. How about Thursday at 10 AM?

Option #2 — It is my goal to understand the "big picture" of where your company is going. This data will allow me to better serve your company. Since you are the chief architect of your company's overall strategy, it is essential that we meet. Also, I would like to provide a technology update specific to your industry. My goal is to build a relationship with your company, not sell you something during our first meeting. I can be a free consulting resource and add tremendous value. Please give me 30 minutes of your time. How about Thursday at 10 AM?

> » **Special <u>Blue Print</u> Tip** — *If you are pushed down to a lower level, make sure to secure the lower-level person's contact information and gain an endorsement from the C-Level (use his/her name) to lock down the appointment with the lower level employee. Prior to ending the call, gain the C-Level's commitment for a future appointment so that after meeting with the lower level employee, you can share ideas about how you can make their company be more productive directly with the C-Level decision-maker. This strategy prevents you from becoming stuck with the lower level person that does not have the authority to make a final decision.*

Before concluding this pivotal chapter, I must SHOW YOU THE MONEY! To effectively demonstrate the power of this necessary evil, I would like to quantify how much money each telemarketing call is worth. We covered this concept in a previous chapter entitled "*<u>The Importance of Time Management</u>*." However, it will be extremely powerful to relate time and money to the task of actually picking up the phone.

Here are some assumptions to calculate the value of each **COLD CALL**:

- Based on making **$200,000** per year in total compensation

- Based on a monthly goal of **<u>32</u>** Customer-Facing Appointments each month

- Main Assumption — **it takes <u>10</u> telemarketing calls to secure <u>1</u> appointment**

- Here is the magic formula:

- How much is each New Appointment worth? — **<u>$521</u>** (*Formula — 32 appointments x 12 months = 384 Total Appointments per year — $200,000/384 = $521*)

- How much is each call worth? — **$52.10** (*Formula — $521 per appointments/10 Calls = $52.10*) — based on the assumption it takes 10 calls to get 1 appointment

Based on this math, each time you pick up the phone and make a tough *cold call*, it is worth **$52.10**. If you are willing to make a minimum of **<u>50</u>** **"cold calls"** per day, you will add **$2,605** to your bank account! So look yourself in the mirror before you start your day and ask the following questions — *Do you want to get paid, do you want to dominate the market, and are you ready to make **$2,605** today (50 cold calls x $52.10)?*

Few people enjoy telemarketing. Nevertheless, it is a crucial activity in the world of professional sales. If you are confident, prepared to handle objections, and exude a positive attitude that permeates through the phone, you can successfully land appointments via the infamous **COLD CALL** on a regular basis.

PART 4
Managing the Sales Process

Chapter 15
Solution Selling vs. Product Slinging
Are you a True Sales Professional or a Product Slinger?

"We have two ears and one mouth so that we can listen twice as much as we speak."

- Epictetus, Greek Philosopher -

One of my close friends taught me an extremely valuable lesson he learned from his father — **"The key to real communication is LISTENING. This is why we have two ears and one mouth."**

This is a vital concept that we need to discuss in great detail. Improving my listening skills is at the top of my New Years Day resolution list every year. Whether it is "actively" listening to my colleagues & clients at work or listening closely to my wife & kids at home, I struggle to master this critical competency.

Sales people love to talk! Many times, we listen with the intent to answer versus listening with the intent to understand. We also have the bad habit of listening to answer the question. What I mean by this statement is that while the person is speaking, we are already formulating our response in our heads and not hearing the full message. Many times, we will even interrupt the person speaking because we are so anxious to share our thoughts. To curb my enthusiasm to talk, I often put two fingers over my lips to stifle my urge to unintentionally interrupt the person speaking. Another tactic I employ is silently counting to ten and resisting the urge to speak until I reach the number 10. These tactics help me listen to the person speaking and give them a chance to finish their point. As a sales professional, I'm confident I am not alone.

Listening is the key to becoming a powerful sales professional; therefore, we should all constantly work to improve. Developing excellent listening skills separates the "GOOD" sales reps from the "GREAT" sales professionals. When you listen to your client, you uncover their pain points, business goals, and personal data, which are the necessary goods required to win deals. When you don't listen to your clients, you miss all of the critical material to build a meaningful business partnership.

The aptitude to listen is one of the main factors to evaluate sales talent. Based on listening skills, we can group sales professionals into two distinct categories. There is the "**Solution Selling Sales Professional**" and the infamous "**Product Slinger**." Both individuals are very easy to identify and produce vastly different levels of sales results.

Before we go any further, we must review the difference between **Solution Selling** and **Product Slinging**. Here is the definition of solution selling:

First you listen and learn how your client makes money and serves their customers. After gathering this necessary data, you help your client leverage your product portfolio to solve real business problems, accomplish primary objectives, make more money, and provide better service to their customers.

Solution selling is an art. It requires intimate knowledge of your client's business objectives and pain-points. This knowledge is acquired by asking brilliant questions with the desire to understand how your client operates. Most importantly, it requires astute listening prowess. If you dedicate time to mastering the art of solution selling, you will always find yourself dealing directly with decision-makers because your client views you as a trusted advisor. Also, you will consistently win strategic sales opportunities because you are solving real business problems. This all leads to consistently making BIG money.

The reverse side of this equation is a product slinger. This individual has poor listening skills and they do not invest time to really understand their client's business operations. Here's how I define this narrowly focused sales professional:

Pushing your product on a customer without knowing how they operate, make money, or provide services to their customers. You are only focused on selling widgets and not really focused on helping your client solve real business problems.

A product slinger is easy to spot. They push their product without understanding anything about their client's needs. If you asked them directly, they will struggle to explain how their client makes money, serves their customers, or what their business challenges are.

Another characteristic of a product slinger is that they ALWAYS sell on price! Since they are not providing any true value, the only thing they can offer is a cheaper price. This is a losing formula especially if the Solution Selling Sales Professional can match their price.

Finally, the product slinger is never positioned at the right level. This happens because they don't offer any true value that would warrant a relationship with a C-Level decision maker. They usually always meet with low level employees with little or no decision making authority. The following phrase is pretty common — *"I need to run this by my boss to get her approval before we can move forward"* — OR — *"Let me ask my boss if we can move forward with your product."* When you sell on price or sling product, you will always struggle to consistently hit quota.

In order to become a solutions selling sales professional that adds true value to your clients, you must master the art of listening. As a courageous person that selected the profession of sales, you have a choice. You can decide to sling product and always scramble at the end of the month to make quota or you can be a solution selling business consultant that builds strong client relationships and solves real problems. Remember, true solution selling requires listening savvy, learning about your client's business operations, and solving true business issues. Solution selling takes more work but I promise it will produce stronger sales results, which leads to BIG commission checks!

Chapter 16
Navigating the Sales Process
From 1st Appointment to Closing the Sale

> *"The winds and waves are always
> on the side of the ablest navigators."*

- Edward Gibbon, English Historian -

Landing your first appointment with a new prospect is very difficult. Now that you have accomplished this significant task, you must effectively manage the sales cycle to close the deal. At times, this complex process reminds me of coaching my six-year-old daughter's soccer team. I am tasked with convincing these easily distracted little girls to stay laser focused on competing, remembering their fundamentals, playing defense, running in the hot Texas sun, and scoring goals. Many times, their priorities are not playing soccer. Instead, they are focused on playing with their teammates during the game, staring at the sky, drinking Gatorade, running to mommy and daddy, and eating the tasty snacks after the game. Also, this arduous task requires cooperation from the child's parents (major influencers), who may not take this activity as seriously as their ultra competitive coach (me) who wants to win the game! Coaching a team of six-year-old girls requires patience, focus, organization, persuasion, and leadership. As a sales professional, navigating the sales cycle poses similar challenges.

Once you land the first appointment and uncover a legitimate opportunity, your number one priority is closing the sale. Unfortunately, this may not be top priority for your client; therefore, it is your responsibility to demonstrate the value of your product, produce a compelling ROI (return on investment), build trust, gain access to the decision-maker, and close your sale. Due to the myriad of challenges you will encounter to move the deal towards closure, you must master the concepts in this chapter to make money!

There are six main reasons why many sales professionals cannot make progress after the first appointment. They are easy to identify but I will take a minute to point them out — *failure to listen and learn about the client's pain points and business objectives, failure to ask the right questions, failure to demonstrate an enticing return on investment (ROI), failure to meet directly with the "real" decision-maker, failure to create a sense of urgency, and failure to determine if a real opportunity exists and not waste time.* The goal of this chapter is to help you avoid these pitfalls.

Preparation, organization, and consistency are keys to effectively managing the sales cycle. Failure to accomplish these tasks is detrimental to your progress. To avoid these pitfalls, you must execute the five phases of the sales process.

Here is a breakdown of these five phases — *first appointment, uncovering the customer's pain points, identifying the opportunity, presenting your proposal, and closing the business.*

I will now provide detailed insight into each phase of the sales process.

First Appointment

Once you land your first customer facing appointment, the clock starts. Everything you say and do will be evaluated. You must be prepared, use all resources at your disposal, and deliver on all commitments. I will now present some excellent preparation tips to complete before attending a customer appointment.

Before meeting with your client, conduct a strategy session with everyone from your company attending the meeting. This will ensure your team follows the agenda, understands their roles, comprehends the meeting objectives, is aware of the topics to avoid, and knows the account history. Also, this action will avoid any wild card situations where your support team accidently raises a sensitive topic, introduces an irrelevant item, or asks a silly question. During this session, you also want to discuss the goals/objectives for the appointment and make sure everyone is on the same page.

Next, you must visit their company website (*if they do not have a website, research them on the internet)!* This provides an opportunity to learn about how the company operates, the performance of their stock if publicly traded, and provide an update on any recent press releases. If you do not take time to learn how your potential client operates, you are wasting your time and you will end up succumbing to the pitfalls we discussed at the beginning of this chapter (*please don't be the "Product Slinger" we exposed in the previous chapter entitled —* "Solution Selling vs. Product Slinging").

> » **Special Blue Print Tip** — *I strongly recommend that you invest in a powerful business tool called **First Research**. This tool provides valuable industry intelligence in an easy to comprehend format that*

will help you understand the challenges and opportunities within your client's respective industry. **First Research** *provides granular data on over 900 industry segments. Also, their database is consistently updated so the information is always current. Finally, this tool is extremely user friendly. You merely input the industry you are interested in learning about and the tool will instantly provide a comprehensive overview of the industry, recent developments, business challenges, current trends, growth opportunities, executive insight (complete breakdown of what each level within the chain of command is focused on), call prep questions (outstanding questions to ask your client during appointments), and financial information.* **First Research** *can make you an industry expert in less than 20 minutes!*

After learning about the company, you must conduct research on the actual person you are meeting with. Check to see if they are on Facebook, Twitter, or LinkedIn (*great way to learn more about their career path, previous positions, likes/dislikes and insight into their personality*). We will cover the many ways to leverage social networking tools in a later chapter entitled "Harnessing the Explosion of Social Networking Tools."

Finally, you need to prepare a formal meeting agenda. This will show your client that you are organized and you respect their time.

Appointment Checklist

Here is a checklist to walk through before each appointment. Similar to a pilot who inspects his plane prior to departure, you must ensure these items are executed before your meeting. This list will set you apart from other sales professionals and demonstrate that you respect your client's time.

Before the Appointment

1. **Create a customized meeting agenda** — include the customer logo, all meeting participants' names and their titles, and the specific meeting topics you intend to cover

2. **Create a tailor-made information packet as a leave behind** — include marketing collateral of your hottest products, the contact data for the members of your account team, your personal value statement, positive facts on your company, etc.

3. **Research your Client** — check their company website, research their industry so you are aware of the specific trends and challenges (*First Research is a great tool to conduct this exercise*), google

the person you are meeting with, check to see if they are on Facebook, LinkedIn, Twitter, etc.

4.   **Conduct a quick strategy session** — discuss meeting goals with everyone attending the meeting

5.   **NEVER SHOW UP EMPTY HANDED** — take a simple gift or food (*coffee mug, doughnuts, cookies, etc.*)

6.   **Schedule Two Drive-Bys in the Area** — research other potential clients in the area (*use the business tools we will cover in greater detail in the chapter on "Powerful Business Tools to Manage your Daily Sales Activity"*) and create customized information packets to deliver during your Drive-Bys along with a creative gift

After the Appointment

1.   **Send a MOU** (Memo of Understanding) — email summarizing the action items and meeting topics. This vital follow-up email must be sent no later than **48 hrs** after the meeting

2.   **Send a Written Thank You Card** — mandatory for all first appointments or meetings where new players are introduced on an existing account.

3.   **Quick Post Call** — include all members of your team that attended the appointment to discuss next steps, assign action items, set deadlines for completion, and provide feedback (*what worked and what didn't work, ways to improve for the next appointment, etc.*)

4.   **Document your activity** — update your CRM (Customer Relationship Manager) to track and document all of your sales activity that took place during the appointment (*we will review this topic in extensive detail in the chapter on "Powerful Business Tools to Manage your Daily Sales Activity"*)

In summary, the following eight tips will help you lead meaningful customer-facing appointments and accelerate the sales process: (**#1**) — always send a MOU after every customer-facing appointment within 24 to 48 hours, (**#2**) — always conduct strategy sessions before appointments, (**#3**) — always prepare a meeting agenda, (**#4**) — be on time, (**#5**) — bring a simple but impactful gift, (**#5**) — take notes during the meeting, (**#6**) — conduct a "post" call with all parties from your company that attended the meeting, (**#7**) — send hand written Thank You cards to everyone that attended the meeting (*only necessary for 1st appointments*), (**#8**) — keep Saleforce.com or whichever CRM tool your company uses updated with all of your sales activity (*we will cover this topic later in the chapter entitled "Powerful Business Tools to Manage Your Daily Sales Activity."*).

Uncovering the customer's pain points

Uncovering your client's pain points is vital to solving real business problems. If you know how/why/where your product or solution can make a difference in the their business operations, you will be able to develop a winning solution to close the sale. In order to accomplish this critical task, you must conduct research about how your client operates, ask the right questions during appointments, listen closely, and constantly demonstrate how your solution will improve how they operate.

Just like a college student who studies for a final exam or a high school student preparing for the SAT/ACT, this phase of the sales process requires homework. In order to help your client, you must intimately understand the following — *how your client operates, how your client makes money, how your client competes in their respective industry, their short term/long term strategic goals, biggest headaches, major projects over the next 12 months, the most important business challenges they face, their focus areas to improve, and the specific personal goals of your point-of-contact and how they relate to their company's overall business needs.*

Asking the right questions will help you discover this essential data. Once you discover their pain points, you will be able to properly position your product.

Identifying the opportunity

Discovering the client's pain points is how you identify your sales opportunity. If you ask the right questions and understand how your client operates, this phase of the sales process is fairly simple.

Presenting your proposal and solution

One of the central phases of the sales process will be the delivery of your closing presentation to the decision-maker and main influencers involved in the final decision. Presenting an impressive story during this short window of time is critical to winning your deal. To ensure you deliver a compelling presentation that flows smoothly and covers all of the necessary points to close your sale, you must include eight essential pieces. I recommend that you use Microsoft PowerPoint as the delivery method for this presentation.

First, start off with an agenda slide that details what you plan to cover during the presentation and confirms how much time the client has allocated for this meeting. Specifically ask the client how much time you have to present (*for example – "I have us down for 30 minutes today, is this correct?*) What if you expected to present for an entire hour and the CEO had something come up earlier in the day and only has 30 minutes? Knowing the amount of time allocated for the meeting will allow you to hit the most important points required to close your deal.

Second, create a slide called **"Review notes from our previous meetings."** This slide will summarize the timeline and give a brief historical summary of your activity with this account. The purpose of this slide is to confirm all of your assumptions and the key facts you uncovered during the sales process. Most importantly, it solidifies the client's requirements and presents an opportunity to see if anything has changed. This slide should contain the following points — *summary of the client's top priorities, overview of the client's current environment, summary of the items in your proposal, and a summary of the client's main concerns/biggest headaches.*

Third, present a slide that provides a corporate overview of your company. This slide will highlight your company's strengths, accomplishments, and leadership position in your respective industry. The purpose of this slide is to ensure the client is comfortable doing business with you firm.

Fourth, present a slide that provides a brief overview of the product, service, or solution you are selling. This slide will present a concise summary highlighting the premier benefits of your solution.

Fifth, present a slide that summarizes your customized proposal. This slide will review your proposed solution and the associated costs. I would also include an ROI (return on investment) on this slide if applicable.

Sixth, present a slide that provides a customized implementation plan detailing how your company will deploy their service. Be sure you detail all of the resources your company will dedicate to their account. Depending on the complexity of your solution, this slide is very pivotal to reassure the client you can flawlessly deliver your product without impacting their core business operations.

Seventh, present a slide summarizing why the client should buy from your company. This slide should be entitled **"Why My Company"** and deliver a concise synopsis of the major selling points of your company. You should map the strengths of your company directly to the customer's pain points and headaches (*detail how your solution solves their business problems*).

Last but most important, present a slide summarizing why the client should buy from **YOU**! This slide should be called "**Why Reggie Marable**" and offer a concise summary of why the client should conduct business with you! Some of the items to highlight are your work ethic, personal commitment to their success, tenure with your respective company or industry experience, your expertise in their respective industry, client references, etc. People buy from people so this slide could be the extra item that sways the decision in your favor, especially if you are in an ultra competitive industry!

> » **Special Blue Print Tip** — *Ask your happy clients to recommend you on **LinkedIn**. This allows them to write nice things about how you impact their business in a positive way. You can create a special slide with comments directly from these existing clients and incorporate their feedback in every formal presentation to demonstrate these powerful testimonials. This is a great way to establish instant creditability with your prospective clients.*

Here is an example taken directly from one of the most successful sales professionals I have ever worked with, Lacie Garrett-Noe (*her personal **Blue Print** testimonial is located in the appendix at the end of this book*). Lacie asked many of her happy customers to write comments on her LinkedIn page. She includes these testimonials in ALL of her customer presentations.

Here is an example of one she uses frequently:

"Lacie has been an excellent all around individual. She has always been great about listening about our company's specific problems and then providing logical solutions tailored to address them. She is definitely one of the best account executives with whom I have worked with."

I encourage you to organize your critical closing presentation in the format offered by the **Blue Print**. This proven formula will help you close many sales and make BIG MONEY!

Closing the sale

In my opinion, this is the easiest part of the sales process. We will extensively cover this critical phase of the sales process more extensively in a subsequent chapter — "*The Art of Closing the Sale*." The key to executing this step is **ASKING FOR THE BUSINESS**!

In conclusion, I see a striking similarity between the sales process and a long cross country road trip with a group of kids. Imagine being assigned the task of driving from New York City to Los Angeles in a car filled with several antsy children and you must arrive in record time without any delays. This lengthy journey is filled with many winding roads, numerous hills to conquer, and many flat highways filled with idle time. To make matters even more complicated, you are driving a vehicle filled with distractions and noise created by the kids in the back seat, all with competing priorities (*some of the children want to visit the beach while the other kids want to go camping in the mountains — please don't forget the numerous requests to use the bathroom!*) Just like the leader of this potentially disastrous trip, the sales professional must navigate similar challenges when managing the sales process. Remember, you are the driver (leader/conductor) of a high performance vehicle navigating the pathway toward success. In order to reach your destination, you must stay focused on executing the five steps within the sales process, asking the right questions to identify pain points, and delivering a persuasive presentation to the final decision-maker. Most importantly, you must **ASK FOR THE BUSINESS**!

Chapter 17
The Art of Closing the Sale

"Ask, and it shall be given to you"

- Matthew 7:7, The Bible -

You have done everything right throughout the sales process. You established creditability with your client, demonstrated how your product can improve their business operations, and presented an affordable price with a strong ROI (return on investment). It is now time to close the sale! This is the most important part of the sales process; however, it has the perception of being the most difficult. Many sales professionals complicate this process. If you follow all of the **Blue Print** principles, it is just a matter of **ASKING FOR THE BUSINESS**.

I equate this part of the sales process to the climax of a mystery movie filled with suspense. In order to keep the eager audience on the edge of their seats, the movie director must skillfully guide the audience through several scenes. Each scene must include powerful acting, subtle clues, mysterious background music, and chilling suspense. If the director can execute all of these components, the audience will be begging to see the climax and learn the final outcome of the movie! This usually ends with astonishing surprise, frightful screams, and long discussions over dessert and coffee about their awesome movie going experience.

Just like a movie director, you must execute certain fundamentals throughout the sales process to close the sale. First and foremost, you need to uncover the client's pain points and major objectives via powerful questioning skills. If you have these critical facts, you will be able to build a compelling ROI, which clearly demonstrates how your product/service will have a positive impact on their business operations.

Next, you must follow through on ALL commitments throughout the sales process. The client is judging your every move and will consider your actions during the sales process the base line for how you will treat them after you win their business. Think of a first date with someone that really peaks your interest. Everything that takes place on the first couple of dates can make a lasting impression (*were they on time, did they genuinely listen to your conversation, do you have similar interests, was it easy to generate conversation, did they dress nice, etc.).* The same logic applies to building relationships with your clients during the sales process. Dropping the ball during the courting process can easily derail your sale.

Another important fundamental is personally meeting with the final decision-maker during the sales process (*the person that signs the contract*). If you do not meet with the person that signs the contract and your competition does, you immediately put yourself at a significant disadvantage and it is highly probable that you will lose. Also, you are putting your faith in the hands of a "middle man" that is not trained to sell your product (*the "middle man" is your main point of contact that does not have the authority to make a final decision but "claims" they are your champion within their company*). Plus, if the "middle man" is not in favor of selecting your company to win their business, they can potentially sabotage your sale.

Finally, it is critical to sell YOURSELF as a benefit and explain why clients should buy from **YOU**. People buy from people and many times selling yourself is the difference between winning and losing, especially if you are passionate about your product and the company you represent. Also, you should definitely communicate all of the resources your company will allocate to their account if they become a client (*emphasize the power of your account team*). If you carry out these basic fundamentals, asking for the business will be easy!

Here are the 10 items on the **Blue Print** checklist that ensure you will close the sale:

1. Can you explain how your product helps your client? — *If you cannot answer this question with a resounding **YES**, you are slinging product and **NOT** solution selling.*

2. Does your product or service solve a business problem or improve the client's business operations?

3. Have you identified and met all of their decision-making criteria?

4. Is the price of your product/service an issue? — *If yes, have you demonstrated why the client should make an investment in your product/service by demonstrating the benefits and how it improves their business (provide a ROI)?*

5. Do you know who your competition is? — *If yes, have you effectively sold against their weaknesses and do you know how your competition is selling against you?*

6. Do you know who the chief influencers are within the decision-making process? — *If so, have you addressed all of their concerns and won them over?*

7. Do you have a personal connection and solid working relationship with your client?

8. Do you have an internal champion, that is, someone within the company that is pushing for you to win?

9. Have you presented your solution to the final decision-maker (*are you meeting directly with person that signs the contract*)?

10. Have you provided your client with positive references from existing customers?

If you have covered a majority of the items on this checklist, you should feel confident when you **ASK FOR THE BUSINESS** that your client will say yes! If you cannot check off at least seven items on this list, you run the risk of your sale being delayed or losing to the competition. If you covered all of the items on this list, then I'm confident you will close your sale and make some money!

<u>Script for Asking for the Business</u>

You have worked extremely hard to demonstrate the value of your product, established credibility with your client, and present directly to the decision-maker. You have successfully checked off all ten items on the **Blue Print** closing checklist! It's now time for the easiest part of the sales process which is asking for the business.

Here are a few simple ways to ask for the business — ***can I have your business, can we move forward with signing the contract today, are you ready to move forward today, and when can we start the project?***

Here is a proven script to use if you are uncomfortable with directly asking for the business or have not designed your own style to accomplish this task.

"It has been a pleasure building a strong relationship with your team throughout this process. I strongly believe we have developed a powerful solution to impact your business operations in a positive way. We have presented a very attractive financial package and detailed all of the resources that will be deployed to support your account. Finally, I am personally committed to working extremely hard to make you successful and build a fruitful business relationship between our companies. Can we move forward with signing the contract today?"

After you ask for the business, **SHUT UP** and let the client respond. If they do not say YES, be prepared to rebut and ask why. Here is an excellent rebuttal:

After demonstrating the value of our solution, I am surprised to learn that you are not ready to move forward today. What concerns do you have about moving forward with me? — **LET THEM RESPOND WITH THEIR CONCERNS**. *And then state: If I address these concerns, will you be prepared to move forward today?*

Based on your client's response to this rebuttal, you will know immediately if they are serious about doing business with you.

Remember, if you have diligently executed the **Blue Print** throughout the sales process, you are entitled to ask for the business and you owe it to yourself! You will immediately know if you are wasting your time or if the client is serious about doing business with you. Please do not be scared to ask for the business! You can help your client improve their business operations, you worked hard to demonstrate the value of your product, and you were professional. You deserve to win the sale so **ASK FOR IT**!

PART 5
Successful Ways to Manage Your Business

Being the CEO of your own business

Chapter 18
Powerful Business Tools to
Manage your Sales Activity

*"Genius is one percent inspiration and
ninety-nine percent perspiration."*

- Thomas Edison, American Inventor -

One of my business colleagues classifies sales professionals into two distinct categories — the **UNORGANIZED Sales Professional** and **the ORGANIZED Sales Professional**. *These sales professionals have disparate characteristics and produce vastly different levels of sales results. Here is how we define each sales professional:*

- **The UNORGANIZED Sales Professional** — *this individual attacks the market by placing a blind fold over his/her eyes, spins around until dizzy, and then starts shooting a machine gun at everything that moves.*

- **The ORGANIZED Sales Professional** — *this individual attacks the market by strategically selecting a specific target package that includes detailed information on his/her target. Using the analogy of a trained assassin, the organized sales professional determines where the prey is located, precisely what time they will show up, and what type of protection and security is available for the prey. This skillful marksman then takes an elevated position with a high powered rifle, and strategically strikes his target with a precise shot.*

The goal of this chapter is make sure you attack the market like an elite Navy Seal with superior training!

As we discussed in a previous chapter on *"Developing and Executing a Contact Plan,"* you must have a system to keep track of your prospecting activity. Leveraging the power of business tools allows you to become the organized sales professional described above.

One of the main fundamentals to the **Blue Print** is staying organized. As a Sales Director responsible for numerous sales professionals, I frequently hear the following comment:

"It is taking me __7__ to __8__ touches before I land my 1ˢᵗ appointment with a new prospect."

If it takes **seven** to **eight** different touches to land your first appointment, it is vital to have a system to organize your prospecting activity. This apparatus will let you know **who** you touched, **when** you touched them, and **how** you touched them (*phone call, email, drive-by, etc.*). If you are disorganized, you will not have a process to make enough quality touches to secure that first appointment. Without an organized system, you could easily waste precious time, become frustrated with the lack of response from the many prospects you are pursuing, and quit.

The Christmas holiday season is my favorite time of the year. Since I was a child, I have been enamored by the magic of the holiday season. Everyone is happy, there is a tremendous amount of positive energy in the air, and it is a special time to spend with your closest family & friends. Even after my older brother exposed me to the reality about the non-existence of Santa Claus at the tender age of eight, I still believe in the magic of this special holiday. As my kids opened their presents on Christmas morning, I evaluated the amazing delivery process implemented by Santa Claus (*keep in mind, I am operating on the premise that Santa actually does exist*). If Santa did not have tools to manage his business, how would he remember the names of billions of kids across the world, what toys they want, if they have been naughty or nice, and how to reach their homes? To help Santa stay organized, he uses an army of cheerful elves to build toys and a group of tireless reindeer to fly his sleigh. Similar to Santa Claus with his army of elves and fleet of reindeer, a sales professional needs special helpers too.

Incorporating magical elves to help manage your business will aid you in many ways. They will keep you organized by creating a surgical system to track your prospecting activity. These helpers will make you astute by knowing WHO you called, WHEN you called them, and WHAT activity you did last. You will work smarter by setting reminders to execute ALL steps within the **Blue Print** (*reminders for making the next drive-by, placing a follow up phone call, sending an email, etc.*). Finally, business tools will allow you to consistently touch your prospect list/existing customer base on a frequent basis. You cannot do these tasks alone so get some help!

There are four areas where business tools will come in handy. These crucial sections are — (**#1**) *building a prospect list*, (**#2**) *tracking your* *prospecting activity*, (#3) *tracking your sales opportunities*, and (#4) *organizing your existing customer base*. I consider these categories vital because they lead to building relationships, closing business, and securing referrals. These areas are the life blood to your business!

I will now elaborate and provide recommendations on tools to use for each category.

Building a Prospect List

The best tools for this task are **Business Wise** (1st), **Hoovers** (2nd), and **Data.com** (3rd). Business Wise is by far the best tool that I have used; however, it is only available in Atlanta, Charlotte, and Dallas/Fort Worth, at this time. They will allow you to build a strategically focused prospect list. These tools will also give you the opportunity to create a prospect list based on the following criteria — *geography (state, city, metro area, zip code, street, etc.), total number of employees (company-wide and at a specific address), total number of sites, estimated sales revenue, public or private company, and by a specific industry or vertical (healthcare, transportation, education, manufacturing, construction, etc.).* These tools give you the ability to drill down further with even more search criteria; however, the features above are the main ones I use.

> » **Special Blue Print Example** — *Let's say I would like to build a prospect list across the Dallas/Fort Worth metroplex that targets all healthcare companies with more than 100 employees. These tools give me the ability to easily accomplish this task. Also, I could even make the list more focused on all healthcare companies in the city of Irving, TX that have between 50 — 500 employees.*

Tracking your Prospecting Activity

A consistent attack method combined with an organized tracking system form the winning formula to successfully penetrate your prospect list. You must know **who** you called, **when** you called them, and **what** type of contact method was used (*drive-by, voice mail, phone call, formal letter, etc.*). There are several tools to accomplish this task. In my opinion, the best tool is Salesforce.com, which is a web-based CRM tool that allows you to electronically store all of your sales activity, run customized reports, and strategically analyze your activity at the click of a button. This tool is available 24/7 via their secure website and can be accessed from a computer, tablet, iPad, or smartphone. I live and die by Salesforce.com. I use this tool to manage all of my prospecting activity by creating an account profile for every prospect and customer that I target. Here is a summary of the notes I load within each account profile — *company facts, who I am targeting including their specific contact information, all* activity *(phone calls, emails, drive-bys, written letters, etc.)*, full prospecting history *(dates and times of who I called and what I did)*, set reminders to complete ALL steps in the **Blue Print** *(for example, after doing a Drive-By, you can send a reminder for a follow up phone call on a specific date/time)*, exact appointment dates *(who I met with and which members from my sales team attended the meeting)*, proposals, contracts, orders placed by the customer, and account history. I could continue for several pages about the level of material that could be added to the account profile. Imagine the power at your disposal if you can quickly access this data each time you touch an account. **Remember** — WORKING SMART is important to being a successful sales professional and making big money! Running your business in this fashion will lead to consistent success.

If your company does not invest in a CRM tool or you cannot afford to purchase a license on your own, you can build a home-grown system by creating an electronic library within your email account (*Microsoft outlook, Gmail, Yahoo, etc.*). If you need to create a home-grown system, you will need to build a folder for every prospect and customer on your target list, store all communication within each folder, and review the notes within these folders prior to touching or contacting the account. This is more of a manual process; however, it will provide the same functionality as Salesforce.com.

> » **Special Blue Print Tip** — *Invest in a zip drive and back-up your email, all personal files, and your computer hard drive once per month. This process takes less than 30 minutes and will save your life if your computer crashes or is lost/stolen. During my first year as an outside sales rep, my computer was stolen and I lost ALL of my data (prospecting activity, customer files, proposals, contracts, etc.). It took me more than 90 days to recover all of my information and rebuild all of my prospecting scripts. I lost a great deal of productivity and momentum. Instead of prospecting for new business, I spent valuable selling time trying to rebuild my extensive library of information. Please learn from my painful mistake and back-up your critical files every month!*

Tracking your Sales Opportunities

Once again, the best tool available is Salesforce.com. You can create the following customized reports to track all pending proposals and ensure you are pushing them towards closure — *30/60/90 sales funnel report (provides an organized view of all pending opportunities within a 90 day time frame broken out by the likelihood of closure — this report can also stack rank your pending deals based on the actual probability to close), top opportunities report (organized view of your top ten or twenty deals), stuck opportunities report (organized view of all delayed opportunities), all opportunities within a calendar or fiscal year (organized view of every opportunity in your sales funnel), lost opportunities report (organized view of all deals you lost in a given time period. This presents a chance to follow up and try to win the client's business again — second time is always a charm).*

All of these reports will provide valuable insight into the operation of your daily business. You will know what deals you have in the funnel, be able to constantly analyze your progress towards closing these pending opportunities, and follow up on lost opportunities, which could be low-hanging fruit if you analyzed why you lost the previous deal. Finally, these reports will help you strategize on ways to push the stuck or delayed opportunities towards closure.

Once again, if you do not have the ability to use a CRM tool, then you can create a home-grown system using excel by creating a spreadsheet with tabs for each of the reports above. You will need to manually input the notes but it will accomplish the same task.

Organizing your Existing Customer Base

No surprise here! The best tools available to manage your account base are Salesforce.com and a customized electronic library system in your email account. Even if you have Salesforce.com or another CRM tool, I strongly encourage you to use both systems. When using Salesforce.com, you merely need to store this data within the account profile. For the electronic library system, you need to create a folder for every account and store all pertinent material within that specific folder (*contracts, proposals, account history, billing data, and email communication*). I strongly recommend that you create sub-folders for all of your large, active, or most vital accounts and store important information. For example, create sub folders for specific topics like contracts, billing data, proposals, service issues, C-Level contacts, and marketing initiatives would be a few example names of sub-folders. This system gives you the power to quickly reference and locate data on your top accounts. Initially, this will take some work but this system will pay dividends!

> » **Special Blue Print Example** — *I have access to EVERY electronic communication dating back to 2003 for EACH customer I have managed, as well as EVERY SINGLE prospect I have ever targeted since my days as a direct sales rep. I cannot emphasize enough how much this level of organization has improved the way I operate!*

In summary, Business Wise Hoovers, Data.com, Salesforce.com, and the home-grown tools we reviewed in this chapter are the best weapons to incorporate into the daily operation of your business. Just like Santa Claus who delivers gifts to billions of kids across the world on a single day, you need help to effectively run your business! Investing in business tools will keep you organized, help you work smarter, and operate like a Navy Seal (*an elite special forces solider with detailed information to accomplish a well orchestrated mission*).

Chapter 19
Harnessing the Explosion of Social Networking Tools

"When you're finished changing, you're finished."

- Benjamin Franklin, American Statesman, Scientist, & Philosopher -

The explosion of social networking cannot be ignored. It has transcended beyond everyone's personal life and drastically impacted the business world. This phenomenon is an excellent way to communicate with and learn more about your clients. These social networking platforms can provide details about your client's career path, personal life, and details about how they market their products.

The social networking sites essential to sales professionals are **LinkedIn**, **Facebook**, and **Twitter**. Here is a breakdown of each site:

LinkedIn

LinkedIn is an excellent social networking tool that is tailor-made for business professionals because it is mainly used for professional networking. This site allows users to maintain a list of contact details for people with whom they have some level of relationship.

The popularity and pervasiveness of LinkedIn cannot be overlooked. It operates the world's largest professional network on the Internet with more than 100 million members in over 200 countries and territories. Roughly one million new members join LinkedIn every week, at a rate equivalent to a professional joining the site faster than one member per second. LinkedIn counts executives from all Fortune 500 companies as members and more than 2 million companies have LinkedIn company pages.

LinkedIn is primarily used for networking, employment searches, and overall research. Users can gain an introduction to someone through a mutual contact and find jobs, people, and business opportunities recommended by someone in their network. This site is also used by employers to list jobs and search for potential candidates. Consequently, job seekers review the profile of hiring managers and discover which of their existing contacts can introduce them. Finally, users can post their own photos and view photos of others to aid in identification, which is an extremely useful tool.

From a sales and marketing perspective, LinkedIn can be an excellent way to learn about customers and prospects. Users can follow different companies and gain notification about the new members who join the company, new products or services, and job offers that become available. Also, people can use LinkedIn as a research tool by learning statistics about most companies listed on the site (*percentage of the most common titles/positions held within the company, the location of the company's headquarters and offices, and a list of present and former employees*).

As a sales professional, there are several ways you can leverage LinkedIn. **First and foremost**, you can research one of your existing customers or prospects as most companies have a LinkedIn profile and usually keep these facts current. They frequently list meaningful data about their corporate profile and many other relevant facts that will educate you on their operations.

Second, you can learn pertinent details about the individual person you are targeting. Most business professionals have a LinkedIn profile and keep this material current. These details will educate you on their career path, previous jobs, other companies they have worked for, and their educational background (*college, graduate school, advanced degrees, etc.*). All of these valuable goodies will help you better connect with your contact.

Third, this site provides another avenue to secure that treasured appointment. You can personally introduce yourself to your contact via LinkedIn or have someone in your professional/personal network introduce you that may know this person.

Fourth, LinkedIn provides a strong platform to tout and market your own personal brand. Many times, your potential clients and customers may conduct their own research about you especially if they are making a significant financial investment in your service. It will strengthen your creditability when you have recommendations from your existing base of customers touting your strength as their account manager or vouching for your product/service. You will need to ask your customers to post a recommendation on your LinkedIn page (*depending on how detailed their recommendation is, this process can take less than 15 minutes of someone's time*).

Fifth, LinkedIn allows you to "follow" and stay current on your customers and prospects. Once you are part of their LinkedIn community (*you will need to send them a connection request*), you will receive all updates that they make to their profile. As long as they keep their profile current, you will stay abreast of everything taking place within their hemisphere.

Last but definitely not least, this site provides the opportunity to maintain and cultivate your professional network. You can stay connected with hundreds of individuals via the click of a button. If you change jobs, receive a promotion, or land a big sale, update your LinkedIn page. Everyone in your LinkedIn network will receive an instant update about your progress. Please encourage everyone you know to stay current and get on LinkedIn!

Facebook

Facebook has become one of the most popular social networking sites in the US with over 600 million active users. An astonishing 41.6% of the U.S. population has a Facebook account and it has the second highest web traffic in the US. It is primarily used for personal networking; however, it can be used to learn about your customers and prospects. In today's society, it is quite rare that someone over the age of 12 does not have their own personal Facebook page.

Facebook has made a major impact on the social life and activity of people across the world. It has reunited lost family members and friends, completely changed the political process (*remember the 2008 presidential campaign*), helped inspire political revolution (*Facebook was the catalyst for the overthrow of former Egyptian President Hosni Mubarak in 2011*), and completely changed how corporations market their products.

There are a multitude of ways that people use this social networking site. People use Facebook to keep in touch with family members and friends, share pictures (*it is the most popular website for uploading photos with 50 billion uploaded cumulatively*), update people on what's happening in their life through status updates, establish an on-line/internet presence, gain an introduction to someone through a mutual contact, and find jobs, people, and business opportunities. Also, people use Facebook to "follow" their favorite friends, celebrities, and companies.

From a business perspective, many companies create business accounts with Facebook and use this as a platform to market new products and services. They also use Facebook to run and manage advertising campaigns. Following a company on Facebook will help you stay current on their latest developments.

Facebook offers several unique features. Here is a list of the most popular features used by their user community — Unique Personal Profiles (*users can create personal profiles with photos, lists of their personal interests, contact information, and other personal material. Via this unique personal profile, the user can add other users as friends, and exchange messages, including automatic notifications when they update their profile*), Frequent Status Updates which allows users to discuss their thoughts, whereabouts, or share important news with their friends (*when a status is updated, it posts on the user's personal wall, as well as in the news feeds of their friends. Status can be updated from a web browser, mobile device, or text message*), Messaging Features (*users can communicate with friends and other users through private or public messages and a chat feature*), Special Interest Groups (*users can create and join common-interest user groups, organized by workplace, school or college, or other characteristics*), and Security features that enable users to choose their own privacy settings and select who can view specific parts of their profile.

As a sales professional, there are several ways you can leverage the capabilities of Facebook. Many of these useful methods are similar to the items we just covered regarding LinkedIn.

First, you can research one of your existing customers or prospects as most companies have a Facebook page and usually keep this information current. They usually always list telling figures about their corporate profile, new products, and many other pertinent facts that will educate you on how they operate. As we discussed earlier in this chapter, many companies utilize the advertising capabilities of Facebook to run marketing campaigns. As a member of their network, you will proactively receive all news related to the companies you "follow" on Facebook.

Second, you can learn pertinent details about the individual person you are targeting. Most business professionals have a Facebook page and keep this data current (*some people update their Facebook page multiple times per day*). These details will educate you on their personal life, interests, hobbies, and their overall passion. You can also learn about their career path, previous jobs, other companies they have worked for, and their educational background (*college, graduate school, advanced degrees, etc.*). Finally, just about every person on Facebook will have many pictures so you will have an opportunity to gain a visual picture of them. All of these fabulous goodies will help you establish rapport and connect with your contact.

Third, this site provides another avenue to secure that treasured appointment. You can personally introduce yourself to your contact via Facebook by sending them a "Friend Request"; however, proceed with caution if you go this route. Some people may perceive this as an encroachment on their personal space outside of work.

Fourth, Facebook will help to maintain and cultivate your professional network. You can stay connected with hundreds of individuals via the click of a button. If you change jobs, receive a promotion, or land a big sale, update your Facebook page. All of your many Facebook friends will receive an instant update about your progress. Please encourage everyone you know to stay current and get on Facebook!

Last but most important, Facebook provides a compelling platform to tout and market your own personal brand. As we discussed earlier, your potential clients and customers may conduct their own research about you especially if they are making a significant financial investment in your service. Since you are a CEO of your own business, I strongly encourage you to maintain a "**professional**" Facebook site. I would not post any photos, comments, or material that could potentially cast a negative light on your personal brand. I am referring to *indecent photos*, *political commentary*, *profanity*, *obscene videos*, *disrespectful wall posts from your Facebook friends*, or *any potentially distasteful information*. Facebook is a powerful tool but it could be a way to immediately eliminate you from future business relationships or career opportunities if your potential clients or employers find your Facebook page unprofessional, disrespectful, or distasteful. I strongly recommend that you maintain a conservative Facebook page. If you do not follow my advice, please use the privacy settings to limit who can view your Facebook page. Trust me, it will strengthen your creditability when you have a professional and respectful Facebook page.

Twitter

Another widely used social networking site is Twitter, which has emerged as an extremely popular site with over 225 million active users. Twitter offers a free social networking and micro-blogging service that enables users to send and read small bursts of information called Tweets. Tweets are text-based posts of up to 140 characters displayed on the user's profile page. Each Tweet also contains a detailed pane that provides additional data, more context to the message, and embedded media. Tweets have become an extremely popular way for celebrities, political figures, and professional athletes to communicate with their fans and how many young adults stay in touch versus sending traditional email or text messages. Twitter currently generates 190 million tweets a day and handles over 1.6 billion search queries per day.

Corporations and businesses use Twitter to quickly share news with people interested in their products and services, gather real-time market intelligence, and build relationships with customers, partners and influential people. Twitter gives business clients the opportunity to directly communicate with an engaged audience in real time.

Most people use Twitter to send updates to their followers called "Tweets" or subscribe to receive other users' tweets (*the process of becoming someone's follower is called becoming one of their "tweeps"*). Tweets are publicly visible by default; however, senders can restrict message delivery to just their followers. Users can tweet via the Twitter website, compatible external applications (*such as smartphones/tablets*), or by Short Message Service (SMS). Twitter allows users the ability to update their profile by using their mobile phone either by text messaging or by applications released for certain smartphones and tablets.

Many corporations and business leaders use Twitter. As a sales professional, the best two ways to exploit the power of Twitter are researching one of your existing customers or prospects to learn more about their company (*most companies have a Twitter account and you can follow them and stay current*) and researching to learn more about a specific person you are doing business with or targeting as a new prospect (*if your client is Tweeting, you can sign up as one of their followers (Tweeps) and stay current on what's happening in their life*).

> » **Special Blue Print Tip** — *Before meeting with a client or calling on a new prospect, ALWAYS review their LinkedIn page. Many business professionals keep this data current and you will learn about their career path, previous positions, etc. Next step is to review their Facebook page. If your client is passionate about social networking and keeps an active Facebook page, you will gain valuable insight into what makes up their core personality (you might even learn some things about that person that may surprise you)! Finally, see if they have a Twitter account. If so, sign up to follow them and stay current on all of their Tweets (become one of their loyal "Tweeps.")! These tools will increase the data you have about your client and help you connect with them on a personal level. Remember, knowledge is power!*

In summary, you must jump on the social networking bandwagon in order to succeed in today's environment. Social networking is now a critical part of today's society and provides a great avenue to stay current with your existing customers and prospects. I challenge you to set up a

Facebook account, follow your clients on Twitter, and create your own personal LinkedIn profile. It is totally cool to embrace technology and ride the social networking wave to success!

Chapter 20
The Power of a Mentor

*"Better than a thousand days of diligent study is
one day with a great teacher."*

- Japanese Proverb -

Mentors have been a critical part of my success. I have leveraged these special relationships for guidance prior to making major decisions in my professional career, advice on my personal life, help with my career advancement, and confidential advice on numerous matters. I have several active mentoring relationships with a wide variety of different professional backgrounds that expand beyond my current employer. These outstanding mentors provide diverse perspectives on life, business, and professional/personal success. Without the invaluable wisdom from these pivotal relationships, I doubt my rise in corporate America would have taken place.

Over the past 10 years, I have consistently maintained mentoring relationships with the following senior level corporate executives that span across many different industries:

John Dupree — Senior Vice President of Sales at Sprint

Matt Carter — President of Sprint's Global Wholesale Solutions Group

Carolyn Rehling — Regional Vice President of Sales at Sprint

Nancy Salisbury — Regional Vice President of Sales at Sprint

Wanda Satryb — Senior Vice President of Customer Care at Sprint

Bill Clement — CEO of Atlanta Financial Group

Ricky Matthews — President & publisher of the Press-Register in Mobile, AL, the Mississippi Press in Pascagoula, MS, the Birmingham News, and the Huntsville Times

Paget Alves — Chief Sales Officer at Sprint

Jim Curran — Senior Vice President of Customer Service at Sprint

Danny Bowman — Former President of Sprint's Integrated Solutions Group

Harry Campbell — Co-Owner of Outlook Partners

Moses Brown — Senior Vice President at Reed Elsevier

Loretta Walker — Senior Vice President of HR at Turner Broadcasting

Ron Frieson — Senior Vice President at Children's Healthcare of Atlanta

My Dad — Retired Colonel/US Army

April Marable — My wife and best friend

I encourage you to have a minimum of three mentoring relationships in your life. These special relationships will allow you to rely on the wisdom and tremendous experience of leaders that have achieved the success you aspire to attain. Their insight will accelerate your professional advancement by avoiding the same pitfalls and mistakes they made as they climbed the ranks. Mentors are also an inspiring source of wisdom and knowledge for career advice, professional/personal development, and profound guidance on big decisions that will have a lasting impact on your professional career. They are a confidential sounding board to discuss issues in your career. Finally, they can also enhance your personal life by helping you maintain balance between your work aspirations and personal life. The most crucial feature of having a mentor is that you will receive candid advice from accomplished business professionals that truly care about you and have your best interests at heart!

I divide mentors into three categories - (**#1**) *external to your company* (*they will provide confidential, fresh, and unique guidance*), (**#2**) *internal to your company* (*they will help you navigate the political landscape of your current employer*), and (**#3**) an *internal sponsor that can help advance your career* (*this dynamic individual is in a position to positively impact your career advancement*).

There are certain rules you must follow in order to select a mentor. Always select someone in a position of significant influence (*mover and shaker*) and at least two levels above your current position. For example, if you are a manager, select a Vice-President or President of a major division. You also want to select someone in a position that can impact the advancement of your professional career whether it is through advice, guidance, or internal sponsorship. Finally, do not select someone on your current level. Your mentor must be someone that is extremely accomplished who can offer valuable advice based on their expertise. You need your mentor to challenge and inspire you to achieve more. It is less likely that a person on your current level can accomplish this paramount task.

Would you take financial advice from someone who has no money or is living in poverty? The answer to this question is absolutely NOT! If you needed financial advice to make a big decision that would impact your financial well being, I'm confident you would prefer to chat with Warren Buffet, Robert Kiyosaki, or perhaps Donald Trump versus someone who is living paycheck to paycheck without any money in the bank. Make sure you apply the same logic when selecting a mentor.

Successful leaders (*the type of folks you want as a mentor*) believe in the power of mentorship and giving back to help others. They too have personal mentors and have leveraged the power of mentorship to achieve success. If you are professional, organized, respectful of their time, and take the initiative to establish the relationship, they are likely to grant you an initial meeting and give you the opportunity to build an accord.

I created two email templates to formally request a mentorship and land your first meeting. These templates are divided into the following two categories — **internal to your company** (*this template uses your company language and provides details about your career background that an internal executive would appreciate*) and **external to your company** (*this template references the connection you have with your desired mentor — where you met them, an article you read, etc. — and provides a high level summary of your accomplishments that someone external to your company can quickly comprehend*).

Internal to your company

Matt,

To introduce myself, I'm a Regional Sales Director in Business Sales. Sprint is the only company I have ever worked for since graduating from college and I have aspirations to become a Corporate Officer. I admire your leadership style and stellar accomplishments. It would be an honor to chat with you a few times each year to leverage your wisdom.

Here is a brief summary of my career background:

- *Received Sprint's 2010 Leadership Excellence Award*

- *My area has achieved quota for 14 Consecutive Months*

- *Overall performance increased 178% Year-over Year from 2009 to 2010*

- *15 Years of Experience at Sprint in Sales Management, Direct Sales, Network Engineering, Sales Support, Network Operations, and Customer Service*

- *Played Professional Football in the Canadian Football League*

- *Cum Laude graduate of Morehouse College, Atlanta, GA*

Once again, I would like to chat informally each quarter to gain your candid feedback on my progress. Please advise which date works best for a brief phone conversation.

- ***Thursday-March 31st*** *— anytime between 10 AM and 1 PM CST*

- ***Monday-April 18th*** *— anytime after 2 PM CST*

- ***Wednesday-April 20th*** *— anytime before 12 PM CST*

Thank you in advance and I look forward to hearing from you.

Best Regards,

Reggie Marable

External to your company

Eric,

It was a pleasure meeting you at the ELC Symposium in NYC. To refresh your memory, I'm the gentleman that asked about balancing career aspirations with a positive family life. We spoke briefly after the morning session.

I was recently promoted to my 1st executive level role at Sprint and relocated my family to Dallas. I would love your insight about my future career aspirations to be a leader in corporate America.

Please let me know what time works best for a brief phone conversation.

- ***Tues-Nov 2nd*** *— anytime after 3 PM EST*

- ***Wed-Nov 3rd*** *— anytime after 2 PM EST*

- ***Friday-Nov. 12th*** *— anytime after 2 PM EST*

Once again, I am merely seeking your candid insight about my plan to earn a corporate officer position at Sprint. Thank you in advance and I look forward to hearing from you.

Best Regards,

Reggie Marable

> » **Special Blue Print Tip** — *If you notice from my email templates, I clearly gave these busy people three dates and times to select from when I asked for this meeting (always 1 to 2 weeks out). As we discussed in the chapter on "The Power of Written Communication," this effective tactic will help you quickly book the appointment with your desired mentor. Remember, you are targeting important people to serve as your mentor. These are extremely busy so make it easy for them by providing three dates and times.*

Do not become discouraged if they do not initially respond to your first request. It may take several attempts before you secure your first mentoring session (*Remember — you are dealing with very busy people so execute the **Blue Print** contact plan reviewed in the chapter entitled "Developing & Executing your Contact Plan."*). If you are respectfully persistent, they will grant you time on their calendar. Once you land the initial mentoring session, if you perform the items we will now review, I am confident this meeting will blossom into a fruitful relationship.

It is your responsibility to develop, maintain, and cultivate these special relationships. Mentors are doing you a favor by offering their unbiased opinions so you must take the initiative. Here are four best practices to properly manage these relationships — (**#1**) keep a list of your mentors (*I keep my mentors on an excel spread sheet*), (**#2**) proactively schedule a quarterly meeting with each mentor (*this can be over lunch, conference call, dinner meeting, or in their office — face-to-face is always better; however, if you are in different cities a conference call will work just fine*), (**#3**) outline the topics you want to review with your mentor prior to the meeting (*big career move, problem with your boss, personal advice, etc.*), (**#4**) keep your mentor updated on your successes (*let them know when you close a big sale, land a promotion, complete a significant project — a simple email works perfect*).

The next item to master is effectively managing a formal mentoring session. Properly running this meeting will guarantee that you maximize this valuable time with your mentor.

Before we cover the basic fundamental items for each session, we need to review the two essential subjects that must be covered in your very first mentoring session. **Number one**, have your mentor provide a complete overview of their career path. This historical account will provide insight about their unique background and adventurous pathway to reach their current role. **Number two**, provide a detailed overview of your personal career path. This story gives them insight into your character, work ethic, willingness to take risks, success, ambition, etc. It will also help you establish creditability with your mentor and guarantee they will invest further in your development especially if they see promise in your aspirations to achieve excellence.

I will now cover a sample agenda format to properly conduct a formal mentoring session. Here are the points to cover in each session: (**#1**) — update on what's going on with their current position, (**#2**) — update on their overall career aspirations (*what is the next step for your mentor in their career path and what are they doing to reach the next level*), (**#3**) — update on the progress with your current position (*projects you are working on, success stories, challenges, etc.*), (**#4**) — update on your personal career aspirations (*cover your short term & long term goals — fabulous method to obtain their feedback and suggestions on your progress*), (**#5**) — review hot topics (*items you need their advice on; come prepared to review specific items*), (**#6**) — review personal topics (*always spend time talking about family and your personal lives*), (**#7**) — Ask how you can help them (*I always ask my mentors if there is anything I can do to help them. Remember — It is not always about you!*).

This format allows you to learn from the challenges and situations they face in their profession. If you selected an influential mentor, they are in a position of much higher responsibility. You can learn valuable lessons from hearing about their thought process/strategy to resolve unique issues.

In summary, mentors can accelerate your overall professional development and help advance your career. Building and maintaining a select group of mentors takes work; however, these special relationships will yield priceless benefits that will have a positive impact on your professional career and personal life.

Chapter 21
Building and Maintaining your
Professional Network

*"It's not what you know but who you know
that makes the difference."*

- Anonymous -

We live in a very connected world. Many times, people within your very own personal network are connected to the decision-makers you are trying to meet through aggressive prospecting. If you can devote time to build and maintain a strong professional network, it will yield benefits. This task is definitely hard work, but will help you sell the easy way, which is through warm referrals.

In order to build a fruitful network, you must invest time to build these relationships. This will take hard work and commitment on your part! Think about the effort required to build a prosperous marriage. There are date-nights, commitment to fidelity, family time, compromise, sacrifice, etc. The same thing applies to strong friendships. You have to hang out together, travel together, go through adversity, etc. These strong relationships always pass the test of time and endure through distance.

The best example I can provide is the significance of investing time to cultivate meaningful relationships with your very own children. I'm not referring to being around them. I'm talking about "quality" time! Spending quality time with your kids between the tender ages of 2 — 10 are the most critical times in their development. This builds strong and fruitful relationships that will endure the test of time. If you don't make sacrifices and spend meaningful time in their early years, it will be extremely tough to catch up once they become teenagers. When they are young, you must plant seeds early (*coach their sporting teams, teach them how to ride a bike, play catch, take them to the park, read them bedtime stories, take them out for ice cream, etc.*). Once they become teenagers, they form their own personalities, develop friendships outside of the family, and live in their own world. Parents that failed to invest time in the early years become strangers, foreigners, and even considered intruders within the evolving world of an immature teenager.

The same logic applies to growing a strong network. It takes time and work! Don't forget, these relationships are with people that need attention. Cultivating your network can help your sales efforts in many ways. Most importantly, they will help you secure "warm" introductions to the main decision-makers on your prospect list.

In today's society, the lines between our professional and personal lives cross paths on many occasions. That being said, you will discover that the people within your network probably have a business or personal connection to the folks on your prospect list and can easily help you secure an appointment. When you are targeting an account, ask the folks in your network (*personal and professional*) if they know the person you are trying to reach or if they know anyone else at that particular company. You will be pleasantly surprised by the end result if your network is strong.

A very rewarding benefit is the ability to help other people. You will be in a position to connect other sales professionals with your existing clients. By doing so, you can help your clients solve business problems and help other sales professionals close more deals. One of the most important perks of a powerful network is the ability to help someone find employment. With so many people out of work, you can really have a positive impact on someone's life by helping them land a new job. Remember, it is not always about you. If you can help someone accomplish their professional goals, the favor will be returned. I am a firm believer that good things always happen to good people!

Finally, your network will help you grow professionally. If you surround yourself with successful and positive people, you can learn from the folks in your network if you communicate with them on a regular basis.

I will now cover six outstanding moves to build and maintain your professional network. If executed on a consistent basis, you will build a fruitful network that yields benefits.

First, make a list of everyone you know. Once you list everyone in your entire network, categorize your contacts based on where they fall in your life. A few examples of categories are personal contacts, business contacts, other sales people that you can exchange leads with, etc. This catalogue of contacts will help you stay organized and know which people to call for special favors, opportunities to help other people, and many other occasions.

Second, devise a tracking system to stay current with everyone in your network. There are two options to accomplish this task. Option #1 is to create an excel spread sheet with separate tabs based on the different categories for the folks in your network (*for example, create a tab for personal contacts then list all of those names and the date and description of your last interaction with that person*). Some of the categories to catalog your networking contacts are personal, internal to my company, external business contacts, other sales professionals, family contacts, etc. Option #2 is to create a folder in your email library system for each person in your network (*for example, create a folder called "Networking Contacts," then create a sub-folder called "External Business Contacts" then create a folder for their name and store all correspondence with this individual in this folder*). We covered this subject in a previous chapter entitled *"Powerful Business Tools to Manage Your Daily Sales Activity."* Please refer to this chapter for additional guidance to create a proficient tracking scheme.

Third, analyze your list and determine which people can help your sales career. A perfect place to begin is creating relationships with other sales professionals. This is an excellent place to start because you may be able to exploit the strong business relationships already in place that these sales reps have been cultivating for years. Also, they are probably already conducting business with many of the companies on your prospect list. Make sure you always approach these relationships with the following attitude "what can I do to help YOU." No one wants to help a selfish person that only thinks about their own well being!

Last but most important, you must dedicate time to cultivate these relationships on a consistent basis. You should meet someone in your network for lunch, dinner, coffee, or happy hour once per week. This will allow you to connect with a minimum of four people per month on an intimate level. If you keep these relationships strong, it will be very easy to call on your network when you need their support.

> » **Special Blue Print Tip** — *On a weekly basis, I challenge you to block out a specific time on your calendar to call three people in your professional network and ask them if there is anything you can do to help them. This simple task will take less than 30 minutes of your time each week and will pay major dividends. When people believe you are there to help them achieve success in their business, they will be more willing to help you when you call for a favor.*

Marriages, romantic relationships, friendships, and strong connections with your children take work! If you invest time to cultivate these precious relationships, the benefits will have a wonderful impact on your life. If you are willing to give your professional network similar attention, it will yield career impacting benefits as well. Once you identify and categorize the folks in your network, it is just a matter of staying in touch and keeping the relationships current. Maintaining a vibrant network definitely takes work; however, it will have a positive outcome on your personal life and professional career.

Chapter 22
Strategies to Gain Visibility in Your Organization & Secure the Next Promotion

"Every battle is won before it is fought."

- Sun Tzu, author of "The Art of War"

If you intend to climb the infamous corporate ladder, you must embrace the following concept:

THE MAJORITY OF ALL POSITIONS IN CORPORATE AMERICA ARE USUALLY FILLED BY THE HIRING MANAGER "<u>BEFORE</u>" THE JOB IS POSTED FOR THE GENERAL PUBLIC TO APPLY

If you are applying for a position and you do not have a relationship with the hiring manager (*they are unaware of your skill set, leadership prowess, aspirations, etc.*)**,** you are fighting an uphill battle. I am not saying you will not secure the job; however, you drastically decrease your opportunity for success. The purpose of this chapter is to provide some solid maneuvers to advance your career. Visibility and exposure are the key ingredients to a winning strategy!

Making yourself visible within your organization is vital to furthering your career and landing the next promotion. If people (*especially the leaders that make the hiring decisions*) are not aware of your existence, talents, or aspirations, they cannot help you.

There are many ways to stand out; however, you must deliver elite results on a consistent basis. Delivering a high level of performance is everything and will separate you from the competition for that lucrative promotion.

Once you have established a track record of solid performance, you must make your intentions known. This can be accomplished by meeting with the hiring manager and clearly communicating your career aspirations. In this meeting, you will discover the qualifications for the position and find out what deficiencies you currently have in your skill set that would prevent you from landing a position on their team. You must be direct and ask the hiring manager questions in order to know where you stand and what gaps you need to fill in order to be prepared for the up-coming opportunity. I also encourage you to meet with the Senior Executives of the department you would like to join. These meetings will provide insight into the strategic direction of the organization, which is helpful to land that precious promotion.

Another way to gain visibility is to emerge as a leader and "go-to" person within your organization. To accomplish this task, you must become a subject matter expert in your department (*the person that everyone goes to for questions, guidance, and direction to resolve complex situations*). Also, I encourage you to volunteer for premier project teams within your company to stand out. You can achieve this goal by asking your manager and the key executive over your organization to allow you to contribute on project teams that help improve the overall operations of your company. You must make your intentions known!

Finally, you need to confirm that your direct supervisor will support your career aspirations. During your formal 1-on-1 sessions with your supervisor, make him/her aware of your intentions to move up. Also, communicate your elite performance results and what you are doing to make "them" look good. During these meetings, you must ask them for constant feedback on ways to improve. Finally, it is critical that you have their support (*a great question to ask — "Do I have your support to advance my career as long as I continue to deliver outstanding performance and make you look good?"*). If you do not have a formal 1-on-1 with your supervisor, take the initiative and schedule one!

> » **Special <u>Blue Print</u> Tip** — *Once you figure out the next step in your career, schedule a formal meeting with the hiring manager of the department you would like to join and learn about their organization, what type of qualifications they are looking for, and what deficiencies you have in your skill set that would prevent you from landing the next position on their team. This tactic allows you to informally interview with the hiring manager long before the position is available and puts you on their radar screen. Also, you will discover what gaps you have in your portfolio and work with the hiring manager to develop an action plan to prepare for the position. If you can accomplish this task, the formal interview process becomes a mere formality because you already secured the job!*

In order to move up, you must learn where you stand and how you are perceived in the organization. Here are some excellent questions to ask the leaders and decision-makers within your company when conducting informal meetings — *how am I currently viewed by our senior leadership team, what is the next step that you envision in my career path, what current gaps do you see in my skill set that would prevent or delay my advancement to the next level within our company, what recommendations can you provide to address these shortcomings, and do I have your support to advance my career as long as I continue to deliver outstanding performance?* These questions will clearly define your areas of improvement. You will also know where you stand if these leaders are willing to provide truthful feedback.

As you formulate your plan to climb the corporate ladder, do not forget to employ the power of your internal mentors and sponsors. Make sure you ask them for advice on ways to effectively maneuver within your organization. Also, ask them for a strong recommendation when you apply for different positions. Remember, if you selected the right mentors and sponsors, they carry significant influence to support your career aspirations. If you have developed a strong mentoring relationship, these people care about you and will be glad to help.

I have used these strategic maneuvers throughout my career. They have been instrumental in facilitating my rise from a customer service rep in a call center to a corporate executive responsible for 80+ employees across 4 states and over $300,000,000 of annual revenue. Remember, you must establish yourself before the job is posted! If you carry out these **Blue Print** tips, I am confident you will land that next promotion.

PART 6

Summary of the **<u>Blue Print</u>** Fundamentals

Chapter 23
Failure is **NOT** an Option
Energy Boost for a Tough Day

"Instead of giving myself reasons why I can't,
I give myself reasons why I can."

- Unknown -

Professional Sales is the **TOUGHEST** profession in the world. You are a ferocious warrior with the courage to have your financial well-being determined by your work ethic, ability to overcome obstacles, and willingness to battle through constant rejection. I admire your bravery!

There will come a point in your career where you "<u>will</u>" reach your breaking point. Professional sales is an extremely challenging profession that will put you on an emotional roller coaster ride. You may experience discouragement from losing a big sale, grow weary from rejection, and succumb to the constant pressure to deliver results each month. When you reach that inevitable cross road, please refer to this chapter for an energy boost!

Positive energy is vital to succeeding in professional sales. If you lack energy and enthusiasm, your clients will not be excited to do business with you. Think about your personal life. Do you enjoy being with happy and dynamic people or folks that are negative and constantly complaining? I'm confident that you would rather enjoy the company of a jubilant and energetic friend over the friend that projects negative energy and causes lots of drama. The same rule applies to business. If you constantly exude positive energy and charisma, it will help you build strong business relationships with your clients. People love warm and enthusiastic people! No one desires to be around a lifeless person that lacks energy.

I have personally tasted defeat in direct sales. If you recall from Chapter 1, "<u>Why Did I Create the **Blue Print**</u>?," I was on the brink of disaster. I was struggling to generate sales activity and was on the verge of complete failure. The pressure to deliver sales results, requirement to make numerous cold calls, and constant rejection had broken my spirit and completely shattered my confidence. I had finally reached my breaking point and was ready to quit. What saved me was my belief in the following three concepts — **Failure is NOT an option, winners find ways to WIN despite circumstance, & you must have the COURAGE and willingness to go F-A-R,** *which means be fearless,* **a**ggressive, & relentless!

I wrote these inspirational reminders on the white board located in my cube for daily motivation. These reminders kept my spirits high and helped me overcome the tribulations of this extremely tough profession!

Failure and rejection are part of sales, so do **NOT** allow these obstacles to discourage you. Here are nine perfect examples of successful individuals who tasted defeat before victory:

Albert Einstein was 4 years old before he could speak.

Babe Ruth struck out 1,300 times, which is a major league record.

Michael Jordan was cut from his high school basketball team.

Walt Disney was fired by a newspaper editor because he "lacked imagination and had no original ideas."

Tom Brady was one of the lowest rated quarterbacks in the 2000 NFL draft and was passed over by 31 NFL teams.

Sir Isaac Newton did poorly in grade school and was considered "unpromising."

Thomas Edison was told by his elementary school teacher that he was too stupid to learn anything. He was counseled to go into a field where he might succeed by virtue of his pleasant personality.

F.W. Woolworth had a job in a dry goods store when he was 21, but his boss would not permit him to wait on customers because he "didn't have enough sense to close a sale."

Winston Churchill failed the 6th grade and had to repeat it because he did not complete the tests that were required for promotion.

These remarkable winners tasted failure but went on to accomplish greatness and inspire millions of people across the world. Please use these positive stories to keep you motivated throughout the day.

There are many ways to stay energized when you are close to your breaking point. I always write an inspirational phrase in a visible place in my office to provide a boost of positive energy. I make these phrases big and visible so they stay in my face each day! Also, I constantly refer to a positive or motivational video clip once a day for an energy boost.

Another factor to staying out of the dumps is to surround yourself with other positive and successful sales professionals. When you are depressed or having a rough day, call one of your peers and ask for a pep talk! You will be amazed by the surge of positive energy they will provide to help you keep fighting!

Finally, a winning attitude will determine your success. You must stay away from negative thoughts and cynical people. I call these individuals "drama queens" and "drama kings." You can see them coming a mile away. When they walk, it feels like a storm cloud filled with rain is hovering over their head and following them everywhere they go. Unfortunately, these pessimistic people are everywhere and always searching for someone else to join their pity party filled with misery. You must steer clear of these individuals as they thrive on sucking away your positive energy. Negativity has no place in your life so avoid the folks that live in a constant state of misery and gloom.

In sales, every day could be "THE" day you discover a sales opportunity that changes the trajectory of your professional career and has a lasting impact on your financial well being! Always remember that you are a fearless warrior with the ability to shape your destiny each day of your life. **EVERY SINGLE "COLD" CALL** you make could lead to a lucrative commission check that changes your life! **<u>YOU</u>** have the talent and ability to make busy and influential strangers give you their time, which leads to long lasting business relationships. Do not allow the daily challenges of sales to discourage you from accomplishing your professional and financial goals.

Ninety-five percent of the world's workforce does not possess the will, courage, and fortitude to put their financial well-being on the line each day. Sales professionals are the life blood of business and you are the most important person in your company! Stay focused, remain positive, and remember that your attitude will determine your destiny!

Chapter 24
Everything you need to know on **ONE** Page

"When planning for a year, plant corn.
When planning for a decade, plant trees.
When planning for life, train and educate people."

- Chinese Proverb -

The **Blue Print** is a strategic process that requires discipline, focus, and consistent execution. If you habitually follow this process, it will increase your sales and help you make more money! Please use this chapter as your quick reference guide to execute the **Blue Print** fundamentals. Here are the **21** concepts you must perform on a routine basis in order to fully take advantage of the **Blue Print**:

1. Understand your **WHY**

2. Perfect your Value Statement

3. Manage your time wisely

4. Keep your written communication short and sweet

5. Develop and implement a **Contact Plan**

6. Make the "**DRIVE-BY**" an integral part of your prospecting strategy

7. Build strong relationships with the Administrative Assistant & Receptionist

8. Do NOT over complicate the infamous "Cold Call" — *use the tele-marketing scripts in this book*

9. Effectively manage the sales process

10. Leverage the power of the "Written" Thank You Card

11. Hone your questioning skills

12. Master the art of LISTENING

13. ASK for the business

14. ASK for referrals from your clients

15. Invest in business tools to manage your daily sales activity

16. Incorporate social networking tools into your process

17. **READ** on a regular basis

18. Cultivate your professional network

19. Find Mentors

20. Climb the corporate ladder by gaining visibility within your company

21. Believe in yourself & always **STAY POSITIVE**

The **Blue Print** has given me and many other winning sales professionals the formula to make **BIG MONEY**, climb the corporate ladder, and dominate professional sales. The **Blue Print** is simple; however, it takes focus, organization, hard work and the willingness to improve on a daily basis. If you embrace and execute these simple concepts, you will reap financial and professional success beyond your dreams!

The Market is Open for Business...

Reggie Marable

Architect of the Blue Print

APPENDIX
THE **BLUE PRINT** EXPERIENCE
REAL LIFE SUCCESS STORIES

Give a man a fish and you feed him for a day.
Teach a man to fish and you feed him for a lifetime."

- Chinese Proverb -

Below are five real life success stories from sales professionals who have leveraged my **Blue Print** to achieve success. These testimonials range from the Vice-President level (*responsible for hundreds of employees and close to a billion dollars in annual revenue*) to the individual contributor level (*direct sales rep*). Also, many of these victorious individuals have used my **Blue Print** to secure promotions to high-end sales positions and management.

Carolyn Rehling
Vice President — South & Mid-Atlantic Region Sprint Business Sales

Carolyn Rehling is the Regional Vice-President for Sprint, responsible for all direct sales channels in the Southeast/Mid-Atlantic region. Her responsibility covers eleven states and also includes Sprint's entire direct sales force that sells to the Federal government. Carolyn has been my mentor since 2005 and gave me an opportunity to prove myself as a Regional Sales Director in July 2009. Here is Carolyn Rehling's personal **Blue Print** Experience:

*When I first began mentoring Reggie in 2005, I saw a sales leader that was extremely focused on success and one who had built a career on fundamentally sound sales practices, now known as the **Blue Print**. Reggie built a legacy of success due to his extreme discipline in executing the fundamentals in the **Blue Print**. I had the opportunity to witness the impact of this method twice; the first when Reggie was a sales manager and again after he was pro-moted to sales director. In his role as director, Reggie immediately raised the bar for acceptable performance by instituting the **Blue Print** methodology with his management team. Reggie taught the basics: the fundamentals of cold calling, discipline of doing what was necessary every day, positioning as a solutions provider, always taking the opportunity to close, and the art of leveraging your network.*

These principles are time-tested and proven. Reggie's ability to reverse the momentum of his teams' performances to successful levels demonstrates his capacity to remove obstacles while challenging his team to be creative in their sales approach. I recommend this methodology for anyone that wants to be successful in a sales career and for sales leaders who want to transform the performance of their team.

Carolyn Rehling
Vice President — South & Mid-Atlantic Region
Sprint Business Sales

Mike Lanwehr
Director of Sales — Southeast Area
Sprint Business Sales

Mike Lanwehr is a Regional Sales Director for Sprint, responsible for all direct sales channels in Georgia, Alabama, Mississippi, and the Gulf Coast. Mike gave me my first opportunity to prove myself in sales management back in Feb. 2006. Here is Mike Lanwehr's personal **Blue Print** Experience:

*The **Blue Print** is a sustainable model for surpassing desired sales results. Reggie's success in using the **Blue Print** to maximize the potential of those individuals on his team is well documented over the three years he was a Sales Manager along with this quick results he's already demonstrated in his new role as Sales Director.*

*As a Sales Manager, Reggie instilled the principles of his **Blue Print** with every member on his Atlanta Sales team which he personally recruited. Within 12 months, Reggie had built a consistently high performing team of nine AE's who delivered over quota results for 36 consecutive months. To complement this feat, close to 90% of his team exceeded quota over this same three year period, including Account Executives with no previous sales experience.*

*With the use of the **Blue Print**, Reggie's team finished #2 in the national 2007 President Circle rankings and then surpassed that milestone by way of coming in #1 in 2008. All of these enviable achievements reinforce the consistency which will materialize when the **Blue Print** guidelines are put into place and acted on.*

*As mentioned, Reggie's success with the **Blue Print** did not stop in Atlanta given the quick success he's now having after incorporating these identical principles amongst his new Area comprised of eight Sales teams across North Texas, Oklahoma, Arkansas, and Louisiana, which is the geography he inherited as a Sales Director.*

I would highly recommend that anyone interested in further strengthening their teams culture in order to consistently reach desired sales goals read this book.

Mike Lanwehr
Director of Sales — Southeast Area
Sprint Business Sales

Joey Polk
Sales Manager
CenturyLink

Joey Polk is a Regional Sales Manager for CenturyLink covering Georgia, Alabama and Mississippi. He manages a team of acquisition focused sales professionals charged with developing new logo business in the region. Here is Joey's personal **Blue Print** Experience:

*I joined Reggie Marable's team with no professional B2B sales experience. He introduced the **Blue Print** and frankly, I thought I could do it my way just as well. I had plenty of formal sales training, so why did I have to do it his exact way?*

*In less than a year, I was at risk of losing my job and was on a formal performance improvement plan (a perform or else plan) and trying to decide whether to quit or stay. Reggie and I sat down and discussed my sales funnel and prospecting methods. I relented and said "OK, I will try it your way." The next year was incredible! The same day we met, I picked 20 top prospects I had had little to no success with and went full force at them. Three quickly became viable and one of those alone accounted for my monthly quota for the next year or so. I went from the bottom to a top performer by simply executing the **Blue Print**. I went back through opportunities thought to be dead and began bringing in huge wins for me and Sprint. Prospects that no one believed I could close, closed and became sources of continued growth and referrals. The recognition for bringing in top, well known logo customers was tremendous. The attention changed my career forever!*

*The **Blue Print** is a simple plan, the key is in the details. Utilizing Reggie's proven techniques, I developed an outstanding reputation with all my customers, even as I moved into the highest end of sales at Sprint then on into management at CenturyLink. Parts seem so obvious, the fact is, your competition isn't doing it. Following the **Blue Print** allowed me to grow my accounts, gain success, make money and be promoted to a National Account Manager position where I continued to utilize the **Blue Print** within my Fortune 500 accounts. It was, perhaps, more critical at the highest end of sales, as penetrating deeper and wider within a company is vital at that level. Today I am ingraining the same game changing philosophies I learned into professionals with a few years to a few decades of sales experience and seeing results! I am proof that the **Blue Print** works in companies with five employees and companies with 90,000 employees alike.*

*I have seen the **Blue Print** work, not just for myself but for those around me too. Under Reggie's leadership, our sales branch in Atlanta went from the worst team in the company to number 1! The energy and success of properly executing Reggie's **Blue Print** is contagious. As team members each implemented the **Blue Print**, competition between us took off. We were proof that "success breeds success" as we helped each other in executing our opportunities. I saw new reps excel and seasoned reps who were painfully average become top performers too. The **Blue Print** can change anyone's success. Our team sent numerous people to President's Club and the average income per rep was almost 200% of what we were expected to make! Everyone who followed the plan has the paychecks to prove it.*

*Bottom line — the **Blue Print** shaped how I do business. Thus my career has taken off and in just under seven years, I went from a new B2B sales professional to being a successful Account Executive to a thriving National Account Manager and then a Regional Sales Manger (leading a team of my own sales reps) — but my story isn't over. Success, promotions, self confidence, income and personal satisfaction — every facet of my professional life has improved because of Reggie's **Blue Print**. More important, the quality of life and the pride in a job well done will change you forever. The only question is, how far will you let it take you?*

Joey Polk
Sales Manager
CenturyLink

Lacie Garrett-Noe
Healthcare Account Manager — Georgia
Sprint Business Sales

Lacie Garrett-Noe is a General Business Account Executive in Atlanta focused on acquiring new logo business accounts for Sprint. She started her career with NO Professional Sales Experience in June 2007 and has NEVER MISSED QUOTA, which is a streak of 54 CONSECUTIVE months! She achieved President's Circle in 2007, 2008, and 2010. She was recently promoted to a strategic sales position responsible for the entire healthcare vertical in the state of Georgia.

Here is Lacie's personal **Blue Print** Experience:

*First, I am honored to be an example of the **Blue Print** and grateful for the knowledge that I obtained to carry with me through my professional career. The **Blue Print** is a clear-cut attitude to help one maximize their sales potential. While the majority can understand the basic concept, the ones who execute this plan will benefit most.*

*I implemented the **Blue Print** when I heard the success story of my direct manager and mentor, Reggie Marable, and I'm confident that my career high-lights will inspire you.*

*I was a recent college graduate with a Bachelor of Business Administration. In addition, I experienced a couple years in an inside sales setting that required me to make hundreds of calls a week to contact potential clients without reaping any benefits of closing the sale or making money. I was in a dead-end job and being overworked and underpaid. When given the opportunity to make a career out of professional sales, I was a sponge for education and soaked up the **Blue Print**.*

*Since I started my sales career at Sprint, I have **NEVER** missed quota! I have exceeded my sales quota for 54 consecutive months while making over half a million dollars in less than 4 years in sales commissions. I achieved President's Club three consecutive years and was awarded lavish trips to Hawaii and the Palos Verdes Peninsula in California. Also, I was asked to participate in an interview with Walter Rogers, President and CEO of Baker Communications, about a segment of "Best Practices of Cultivating Commitment."*

*Reggie's **Blue Print** recently helped me achieve a prestigious promotion into Sprint's Public Sector organization with subject matter expertise on Georgia's healthcare market. My competitive advantage during the interview process* was my ability to follow a prospecting regimen that delivered results, *The* **Blue Print**!

You could call my success "luck" if you would like, but like the famous Roman philosopher Seneca says — "Luck is what happens when preparation meets opportunity." My preparation was executing the **Blue Print**!

Lacie Garrett-Noe
Healthcare Account Manager — Georgia
Sprint Business Sales

Paul Reese
Client Executive
Sprint Business Sales

Paul Reese is a Client Executive for Sprint's marquee Fortune 100 Accounts in Atlanta. He manages two of Sprint's largest customers that bill over $250 million in annual revenue. Here is Paul's personal **Blue Print** Experience:

Reggie Marable's **Blue Print** *offers a proven, step-by-step process for envisioning, defining, creating, and maintaining sales success!*

I began working with Reggie when he started his sales career as a Sprint General Business Sales Rep. In my role at the time as a Data Sales Manager, I joined many account reps during client meetings. Because I worked with 8 different AE's, I was able to see both great approaches and lacking attempts. Reggie stood out uniquely because of the system that he created and perfected.

In my opinion, Reggie developed this framework for successful selling because of two inherent traits — a burning desire to succeed and a disciplined work approach that adopted successful techniques, and discarded all ineffective work habits.

He later used this **Blue Print** *to dominate sales and overshadow the performance of even the most seasoned sales executives. Reggie Marable's approach to sales activity is unique in the industry:*

- *His cold calls were planned and impactful, and he envisioned those calls getting him the meetings that he wanted* **before** *he picked up the phone.*

- *His pre-meeting preparation included a* **clear vision of success** *(I personally view this as the most important aspect of sales execution).*

- *Reggie understood what to present, how to deliver the information, and how to* **Listen** *— then adapt his approach on the fly.*

- *Once engaged, it's all about WORK. Work hard for the client, hard for Sprint, hard for yourself. This is the type of work ethic that clients respond to.*

It became clear to me that Reggie's sales approach could be used as a framework for successful selling. I was able to use these valuable lessons in my transition from Data Sales Manager to National Account Manager, and the benefits of this learning continue in my current role now as a Client Executive to our strategic Fortune 100 accounts.

My personal success has been enhanced by learning from Reggie. I work with our largest and most challenging customers, and have grown one such Fortune 100 client from 30,000 subscribers in 2004, to now 280,000+ subscribers and growing (this in spite of the fact that the company only has 193,000 full time employees!). Although my client's company is only half the size of some of our largest customers, my team is doing twice as many subscriber additions as those other accounts on a continuous, month-over-month basis.

*In the last two years alone, we've grown subscriber additions from an already impressive 2,000 subscriber additions / month to **an astonishing 6,000 subscriber additions per month for an impressive 12 months running!** As of December 2010, we are projected to do a record 8,000 activations in 1 month for the two accounts that I manage.*

*Reggie Marable's **Blue Print** can teach sales executives in any industry to <u>envision success first, then execute like no other</u>. Thanks Reggie!*

Paul Reese
Client Executive
Sprint Business Sales

CPSIA information can be obtained
at www.ICGtesting.com
Printed in the USA
LVHW101939070522
718111LV00037B/270